PIVOT POINT FUNDAMENTALS™: COSMETOLOGY

SKIN

© 2016 Pivot Point International, Inc.
All rights reserved.
ISBN 978-1-940593-50-0

1st Edition
3rd Printing, June 2019
Printed in Hong Kong

Pivot Point International, Inc.
Global Headquarters
8725 West Higgins Road, Suite 700
Chicago, IL 60631

847-866-0500
pivot-point.com

26

CONTENTS

112 // SKIN

2

115

65

86

SKIN
THEORY
112.1

EXPLORE //

Has someone ever given you a tip to improve your skin care that really worked?

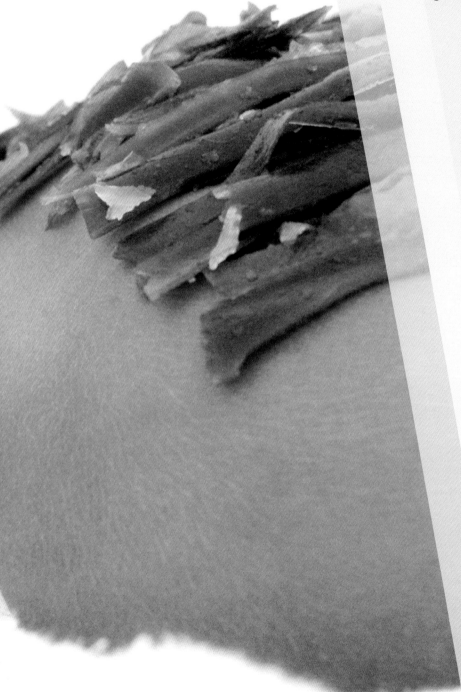

INSPIRE //

Just imagine the appreciation a client would have if you helped their skin become healthy, glowing and attractive.

ACHIEVE //

Following this lesson on *Skin Theory,* you'll be able to:

>> Define the six basic functions of the skin

>> Describe the main composition of the skin

>> Offer examples of how to protect the skin by reducing the sun's harmful effects

>> Explain the basic types of skin surfaces

FOCUS //

SKIN THEORY

Functions of the Skin

Composition of the Skin

Skin Pigmentation and Sunscreen

Types of Skin

112.1 | SKIN THEORY

Amazing Facts About Skin

» An average adult's skin spans 21 square feet, weighs 9 pounds and contains more than 11 miles of blood vessels.

» Your skin sheds 30,000 to 40,000 cells every minute.

» Every month, the entire outer surface of your skin is replaced—a "new you" every 4 weeks. That's almost 1,000 new skin coverings in a lifetime.

» Every square inch of skin holds up to 300 sweat glands.

The skin is the largest—and perhaps most magnificent—organ of the body. It is simultaneously sensitive and supremely durable and requires special attention and care to maintain its health, elasticity, color and vibrancy.

The study of the skin, its structure, functions, diseases and treatment is called **dermatology**. A dermatologist is a medical skin specialist. As a salon professional, it is important for you to have a basic understanding of skin and the skin care services offered in the salon. In the industry, **esthetics** is known as the process of cleansing, toning, moisturizing, protecting and enhancing the skin.

The **skin**, as the largest organ of the body, covers the entire body and protects it from invasion from outside particles. Except for the brain, the skin is also the most complex organ of the body. Your skin is continuously working in its own efficient manner as an intermediary between your body and your environment, performing many functions. The skin and its layers make up the integumentary (in-teg-u-**MEN**-ta-ry) system of the body.

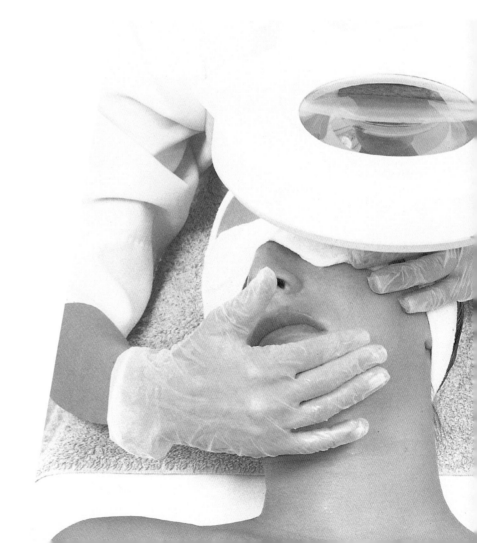

FUNCTIONS OF THE SKIN

The skin is a differentiated structure comprised of cells and tissues that perform specific functions. The skin has six basic functions: sensation, heat regulation, absorption, protection, excretion and secretion. You can use the first letter of each function to spell the word "shapes" which can help you remember the six functions.

SENSATION
Feelings generated by tactile nerve endings just under the outer layer of the skin make you aware of heat, cold, touch, pain and pressure. The reaction to a sensation is called a **reflex**.

HEAT REGULATION
The skin helps control our body temperature so that it maintains our internal heat regardless of environmental climate. It does this through the excretion of sweat from the sudoriferous glands and the dilation of the blood vessels in the dermal layer.

ABSORPTION
The skin permits certain substances like water and oxygen to pass through its tissues. The skin is also able to absorb some oil or fat-based substances on a topical level, but deeper penetration is confined to either medication or application of a water-based substance by means of galvanic current. Penetration of cosmetic preparations is restricted to the epidermal layers only.

PROTECTION
The skin protects the body against blows and falls and direct impact of heat and cold through the fat cells in the subcutaneous tissue. A layer of the skin called the stratum corneum acts as a barrier against bacterial invasion. Another layer called the stratum basale produces melanin pigment as a natural protection or first line of defense against harmful ultraviolet light and environmental pollutants.

EXCRETION
The skin eliminates sweat, salt and wastes from the body, helping to remove toxins from the internal systems and regulate temperature.

SECRETION
The skin secretes **sebum**, a complex mixture of fatty substances that keeps it soft, supple and pliable. The sebum on the skin combines with moisture from the sweat glands to create the acid mantle, which serves as a protective barrier to prevent bacteria from invading the skin and affects the skin's pH level. A sufficient amount of sebum on the skin helps to maintain a normal pH range of 4.5-5.5.

COMPOSITION OF THE SKIN

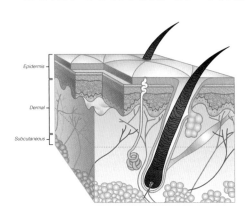

The skin is composed of three main layers:

1. **Epidermis**
   >> Also called cuticle or scarf skin

   >> Outermost layer of the skin

   >> Consists of keratinized surface layers

2. **Dermal**
   >> Also called dermis, derma, corium, cutis or true skin

   >> Underlying, or inner, layer of the skin

   >> Made up primarily of collagen (80%) and elastin (connective tissue, 3%) with sebaceous glands, apocrine glands, eccrine glands and hair follicles

   >> Referred to as the living layer because anything that penetrates the dermal layer is absorbed into the blood and lymph supply

3. **Subcutaneous**
   >> Also called hypodermis, adipose, subcutis, subdermis

   >> Located below the dermal layer

   >> Made up mostly of adipose (fatty) and loose connective tissue and blood vessels

EPIDERMIS

The **epidermis**, also known as the cuticle or scarf skin, makes up the outermost layer of the skin, visible to the eye. It's almost like a bag that covers you and protects you from the environment. Known as the protective layer, the primary function of the epidermis is to keep the insides in and the outside out.

>> There are no blood vessels found in the epidermis, which receives nourishment from the layer below it, the dermal (dermis).

>> The epidermis is primarily composed of **keratinocytes**, also called corneocytes; these consist of the protein keratin and **epithelial cells**, which cover and protect the inside of the body.

>> The epidermis has five layers of cells with differing characteristics: stratum basale, stratum spinosum, stratum granulosum, stratum lucidum and stratum corneum.

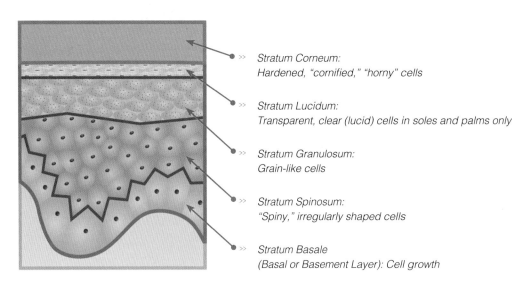

>> *Stratum Corneum:*
Hardened, "cornified," "horny" cells

>> *Stratum Lucidum:*
Transparent, clear (lucid) cells in soles and palms only

>> *Stratum Granulosum:*
Grain-like cells

>> *Stratum Spinosum:*
"Spiny," irregularly shaped cells

>> *Stratum Basale*
(Basal or Basement Layer): Cell growth

The suffix "cyto" and its variant, "cyte" mean cell. They are derived from the Greek term "Kytos," which means hollow container or cell.

Stratum Basale

The **stratum basale**, also called the stratum germinativum, is the lowest or deepest level of the epidermis. Skin cell growth occurs here through mitosis, or cell division. Basal cells are constantly dividing and producing new cells that are pushed toward the surface of the skin to replace cells that have been shed.

>> Keratinocytes in this layer transport cholesterol to the stratum corneum to form a part of the natural moisturizing factor (NMF), which gives the stratum corneum its water binding properties.

>> Melanocytes are found in the stratum basale. These cells produce the melanosomes or pigment granules containing melanin that give color to the skin. Melanin protects the skin, particularly in layers closest to the surface, by screening out harmful ultraviolet (UV) rays.

>> This is the layer involved in basal cell carcinoma (type of cancer).

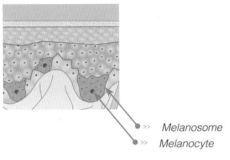

>> *Melanosome*

>> *Melanocyte*

MELANOCYTES

The key function of the melanocyte is to produce a biological pigment, known as melanin, for protection. The structure of the melanocyte is like an octopus with arm-like protrusions called dendrites. These spidery projections extend into the surrounding keratinocytes and deliver melanosomes, which are like packets of melanin.

>> One melanocyte will provide pigment to about 36 keratinocytes.

>> Melanocytes are confined to the basal layer. Sometimes they hang from the epidermis into the dermal layer.

>> Melanocytes in sun-exposed epidermis are larger and have more dendrites than those in epidermis of sun-protected skin. If exposed to UV, the melanocytes increase in size and the dendrites branch.

PIGMENTATION DESCRIPTION

Consider pigmentation or melanin in two categories. The first category would be the basic melanin that has been genetically inherited (what you are born with). The second category to consider is called **hyperpigmentation,** which is pigmentation that occurs as a result of variables such as overexposure to UV rays, acne, injuries to the skin, hormones or other external factors. In skin that may have suffered trauma, the healing process includes the stimulation of melanin-forming cells creating dark spots, which is a form of hyperpigmentation.

Stratum Spinosum

The **stratum spinosum** is the next layer up and is sometimes considered to be part of the stratum basale.

>> It includes cells that have absorbed melanin to distribute pigmentation to other cells.

>> The cells then become irregularly shaped and have connections that appear as spines between the cells that help hold the cells together.

Stratum Granulosum

The next layer is the **stratum granulosum**. In this layer the cells become more regularly shaped and look like many tiny granules. These granules (almost dead cells) are on their way to the surface of the skin to replace cells that are shed from the stratum corneum.

» **Keratinization**, the chemical conversion of living cells into dead protein cells, begins when the newly produced cells are pushed toward the surface.

» The keratinocytes within this layer produce large quantities of protein substances, such as keratin.

Once the keratin is made, it begins forming fibers. The tightly interlocked cells filled with keratin fibers are surrounded by keratohyalin, a protein substance that forms keratin.

» As the newly produced cells move toward the surface and farther away from the stratum basale, they flatten out, lose most of their water, die and, as keratinized cells, are finally shed.

» With the creation of keratin in this layer, one of the functions of the skin—protection—begins.

Stratum Lucidum

The **stratum lucidum** is located on the palms of the hands and the soles of the feet only, where there are no hair follicles.

» Cells found in this layer are even more flattened and transparent (clear) and are called squamous (**SQUAW**-mus) cells due to their flat, scale-like appearance.

» Squamous cells make the skin thickest on the palms of hands and soles of the feet.

» This layer helps reduce friction between the stratum corneum and stratum granulosum.

Stratum Corneum

The uppermost layer, the **stratum corneum** (sometimes called the horny layer) is the toughest layer of the epidermis and is composed of keratin protein cells that are continually shed and replaced by new cells from below.

» Unlike the hard keratin found in nails and hair, the keratin produced by the skin remains soft throughout the keratinization process.

» Squamous cells help this layer act as a protective layer for the layers below it. The stratum corneum protects the skin's moisture balance by acting as a barrier to moisture loss. This mix of moisture balance and cells is called the **barrier function**.

» The stratum corneum is protected by an acid mantle—a mixture of oil secreted by sebaceous oil glands and water secreted by sweat glands. The pH of the acid mantle averages 4.5-5.5.

» Since the skin cells are constantly being sloughed off at the stratum corneum, the replacement of the cells is a continuous process.

» At the very top of this layer is an outer few shell layers of dead epidermal cells called the stratum disjunctum. This is the layer that is exfoliated during skin care services.

The entire epidermis protects the dermal and subcutaneous layers below it. The journey from the stratum basale to the stratum corneum takes between 12 and 19 days during puberty; from 28-35 days during mid-life; and up to 90 days at maturity, depending mostly on the area of the body, age and/or health of the individual.

DERMAL

Unlike the epidermis that is mostly composed of keratinized cells, the **dermal layer** is often called the dermis, derma, corium (**KOH**-ree-um), cutis or true skin because it is the layer of skin that is completely alive. The dermal layer is 25 times thicker than the epidermis and nourishes the lower epidermis. The dermal layer is made up of connective tissues that are composed of a semifluid substance containing collagen protein and elastin fibers, both of which lend support to the epidermis and give the skin its elastic quality.

The dermal layer has two layers: the papillary and the reticular. These layers nourish the epidermis and connect the dermal layer to the layer below it, the subcutaneous layer.

>> The **papillary** layer lies directly beneath the epidermis.

  - It is rich in blood vessels and capillaries, which provide nutrients to the upper layer.

  - From the papillary layer, finger-like projections of the dermal layer extend into the epidermis and nourish the skin.

  - **Tactile corpuscles** (**TAK**-tile **KOR**-pus-uls), types of nerve endings responsible for sensitivity to light touch, are found here within the dermal papillae (**DUR**-mul puh-**PIL**-eye), which are small, nipple-like extensions of the dermal layer into the epidermis; they appear as epidermal or papillary ridges (fingerprints) and are located at the base of hair follicles.

>> The **reticular** is the lowest layer of the dermal layer, and is in direct contact with the next layer of skin, the subcutaneous layer. The reticular layer contains fewer blood vessels. This layer contains the collagen and elastin fibers that provide the skin with its strength and flexibility.

  - Collagen protein fibers are strong and flexible, while the elastin fibers are soft and pliable.

  - It is in this layer that the collagen and elastin fibers deteriorate, causing the skin to sag and wrinkle during the aging process.

Also found in the reticular layer are the sudoriferous (soo-dohr-**IF**-er-us) glands (sweat glands), sebaceous (sih-**BAY**-shus) glands (oil glands), sensory nerve endings and receptors, blood vessels, arrector pili muscles, and a major portion of each hair follicle. Remember that hair is an appendage of the skin, as are the nails and sweat and oil glands.

DISCOVER**MORE**

Epidermal Ridges

The keratinocytes of the stratum lucidum contain densely packed clear keratin. These thick skin areas are where epidermal ridges or whorls are located that provide your palms and soles with traction. You can grasp things with your hands more easily because of these ridges, and they cause friction so you don't slip when walking.

These genetically determined ridges on your fingertips are fingerprints, which have been used for more than a century in crime detection. Your fingerprints are unique and consistent; they do not change as you age. At the time of your birth, ink prints were probably made of epidermal ridges on the soles of your feet for identification purposes.

You can see your own unique set of epidermal ridges or fingerprints. Use a piece of clear tape about 2" (5 cm) long. Stick one end of the tape on your index finger at the fold (skin crease) nearest the tip of your finger. Pull the tape over the top of your index finger to the nail. Firmly press the tape to the fleshy side of your index finger. Carefully remove the tape. Hold the piece of tape up so that a light can shine through it. The image that you see on the tape is the unique fingerprint of your index finger. Each finger and thumb has its own individual "print."

Sudoriferous Glands

The **sudoriferous** (sweat) glands, also called eccrine glands, are duct glands controlled by the nervous system of the body. Each gland consists of a coiled base and tube-like duct opening on the surface of the skin to form a sweat pore. Sweat, the amount of which varies with your body temperature and activity, is a weak salt solution. Besides water and salt, sweat contains other substances that include lactic acid and uric acid, both of which help create the acidic pH of sweat. The sudoriferous glands are widely distributed over the body surface and found in the greatest concentration on the palms of the hands, soles of the feet, scalp and forehead, underarms, anterior trunk and genital region.

The sweat glands have three major functions:

1. **Control and regulation of body temperatures** – When the body becomes overheated, large quantities of sweat are secreted onto the skin's surface. This allows for rapid evaporation, which cools the skin and maintains the body temperature at 98.6°F (37°C).

2. **Excretion of waste products** – Waste materials, such as salt and other chemicals, are easily eliminated as sweat is produced.

3. **Helping to maintain the acidic pH factor of the skin** – A mixture of sweat and oil (acid mantle) keeps the surface of the skin slightly acidic, which helps prevent bacteria from entering the body.

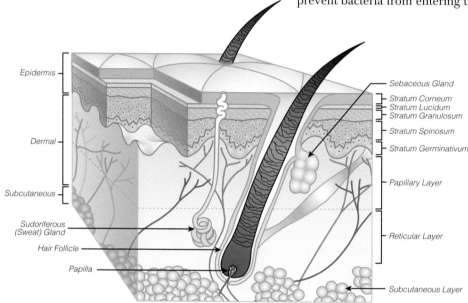

Epidermis
Dermal
Subcutaneous
Sudoriferous (Sweat) Gland
Hair Follicle
Papilla

Sebaceous Gland
Stratum Corneum
Stratum Lucidum
Stratum Granulosum
Stratum Spinosum
Stratum Germinativum
Papillary Layer
Reticular Layer
Subcutaneous Layer

Sebaceous Glands

Sebaceous, or oil, glands are partially controlled by the nervous system and appear as sac-like glands that are attached to hair follicles. These glands are two to three times larger around facial hair follicles than they are around scalp follicles. When sebaceous glands produce an overabundance of sebum, the result is oily skin. No oil glands are found on the palms of the hands or the soles of the feet.

Sebum is a complex secretion containing a high percentage of fatty, oily substances. The sebum mixes with the secretion of the sweat glands and spreads over the surface of the skin. It is this layer of oil and moisture that is called the acid mantle.

>> The acid mantle keeps the skin smooth, prevents dirt and grime from entering the outer layer of the epidermis, and also prevents the skin from drying or chapping.

>> When we measure the pH of the skin, we are actually measuring the pH of the acid mantle.

>> The acid mantle is naturally acidic, ranging from a pH of 4.5-5.5 for most people. This is mainly due to lactic acid and sodium salt.

>> The mantle protects against bacterial invasion by providing a hostile (acidic) environment for bacterial growth.

Most of the problems encountered with skin are caused by the sebaceous gland, whether by underactivity or overactivity or blockage of the duct.

The sebaceous glands are attached to the upper third of the hair follicles and the oil, or sebum, is secreted onto the surface of the skin by way of the papillary (**PAP**-e-lair-y) canal.

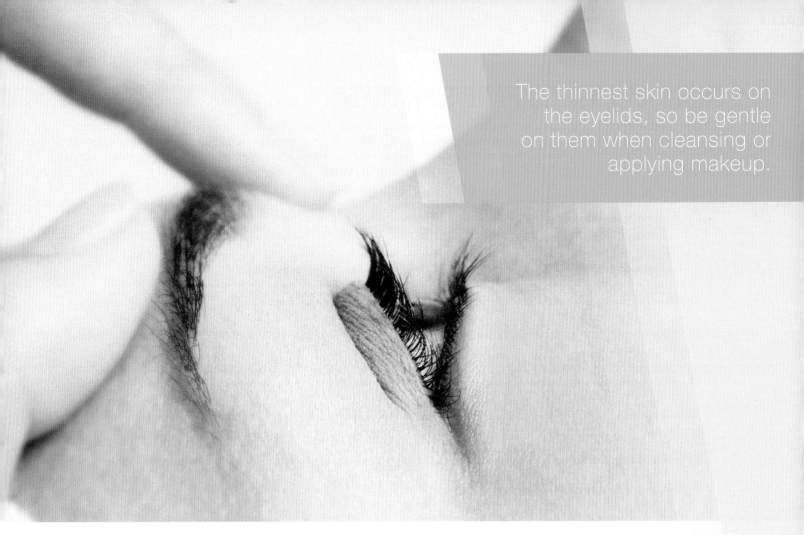

SUBCUTANEOUS

Below the dermal layer of the skin is an adipose (fatty) tissue layer called the **subcutaneous**. The subcutaneous tissue is a protective cushion for the skin. It acts as a shock absorber to protect the bones and to help support the delicate structures, such as blood vessels and nerve endings. This layer gives contour and shape to the body and acts as an emergency reservoir of food and water. It is composed of adipose (fatty) and loose connective tissue.

» The collagen and elastin fibers that run in all directions are continuous with those in the dermal layer.

» Depending upon genetics, nutrition, exercise and general health of the body, varying amounts of fat cells are found in the subcutaneous tissues.

▪ This fatty tissue provides insulation, acts as padding and stores energy for the body. Subcutaneous fat storage is partly under the control of sex hormones, which account for some of the differences in body contours between males and females.

» The subcutaneous layer contains large blood vessels that transport nourishment to the skin and nerves.

» Also in this layer are the glandular parts of some of the sudoriferous glands and some sense organs for touch, pressure and temperature.

» Nerves of the skin are found in the subcutaneous layer and in the lower epidermal layer. Nerve bundles found in the subcutaneous tissue branch into the stratum granulosum layer and respond to pain. Cold, heat and touch affect other nerves, located in lower levels of the epidermis.

SKIN PIGMENTATION AND SUNSCREEN

Melanin-producing cells called melanocytes are located in the basal layer of the epidermis. These cells, loaded with melanin (pigment), move toward the surface at a faster rate than other cells. Melanin is distributed throughout all epidermal cells and forms an effective barrier from the penetration of ultraviolet (UV) rays to the deeper layers of the skin. There are two types of melanin: eumelanin is brown/black in color and pheomelanin is red/yellow in color.

SKIN PIGMENTATION FAST FACTS

>> The amount and type of melanin present along with genes in the human body will determine the type of melanin produced by the melanocytes and the size and distribution of the melansomes in the epidermis.

>> Skin tanning is a result of accelerated melanin production to protect the skin from UV rays.

>> The stimulation of the production of melanin and the tanning of the skin that results also protects the dermal layer by absorbing UV rays.

>> Overexposure to sun can cause damage to the skin, such as burning, peeling, premature aging, freckles and even skin cancer.

>> Light and dark skin do not differ in the number of melanocytes they contain. They differ in the amount and type of melanin produced.

   ▨ Brown skin, which serves as a more effective barrier to the damaging rays of the sun, contains a large amount of melanin.

   ▨ Skin with little melanin will appear pale or pinkish.

   ▨ The "pink" tone visible in pale skin is the reflection of red blood through the epidermis.

   ▨ Carotene, a yellow pigment located primarily in the top layer, can give skin a sallow or yellowish cast. No matter what color, all skin needs protection from the ultraviolet rays of the sun.

>> 1 in 10 cells is a melanocyte (pigment cell).

SUNSCREEN DESCRIPTION

>> Many products have been developed to protect the skin from UV rays. One such product is sunscreen, which comes in various **Sun Protection Factor (SPF)** strengths.

   ▨ SPF represents a sunscreen's ability to shield against the sun's shortwave, ultraviolet B (UVB) rays and delay sun-induced burning or erythema. It measures the length of time a product prevents skin reddening from UVB compared to how long the skin takes to redden without protection. However, SPF does not measure protection against the sun's long-wave, UVA rays, which accelerate skin aging and are strongly implicated in skin cancer along with UVB.

   ▨ The SPF is measured by how long it takes an individual to feel or show erythema (reddening) when exposed to UVB rays. If it is in 10 minutes and you apply a product with an SPF 30, you should be able to withstand exposure to the sun for (10 x 30) 300 minutes, or five hours.

   ▨ This rating system allows you to determine how long you can stay out in the sun without burning.

SUNSCREEN FAST FACTS

>> Sunscreen use needs to coincide with hours of daylight, regardless of cloud coverage, sunny skies or duration outdoors.

>> Try to keep out of the sun between 10 a.m. and 2 p.m. Stay in the shade whenever possible.

>> Damaging UVA and UVB rays can penetrate windows, car windshields, clothing and layers of clouds.

>> Use a sunscreen product with ingredients that block all UVA: zinc oxide, avobenzone and/or butyl methoxydibenzoylmethane.

>> Studies show 90% of wrinkles are caused by excessive exposure to the sun, and only 10% by the natural aging process. If you have had repeated sunburns, examine your skin monthly. If you see a change in the size, shape or appearance of a mole, see your dermatologist.

>> The American Academy of Dermatology recommends the following tips to reduce the sun's harmful effects:

  ▪ Apply a sunscreen with an SPF of at least 30, and reapply every 2 hours.

  ▪ Wear protective, tightly woven clothing.

  ▪ Avoid surfaces, such as water, that can reflect up to 85% of the sun's damaging rays.

  ▪ Protect children by keeping them out of the sun and, beginning at 6 months of age, minimize risk by applying sunscreen. Children younger than 6 months should not be exposed to the sun, since their skin is highly sensitive to the chemical ingredients in sunscreen as well as to the sun's rays. Shade and protective clothing are the best ways to protect infants from the sun.

DISCOVER**MORE**

Sensitive Versus Sensitized: The Genetic Difference

Millions of people perceive their skin as sensitive. In reality, there is sensitive skin (a genetic trait) and there is sensitized skin, a growing phenomenon worldwide caused by increased exposure to pollution, stress and chemicals. The growing number of people affected by sensitization has spurred cosmetic and pharmaceutical industries to develop new products to help combat the reactions triggered by this condition.

A true sensitive skin condition is caused by a genetic predisposition. Someone who is truly sensitive is born with this condition and tends to be prone to blushing, asthma and allergies. This skin is considered more delicate with a lower amount of pigment, a thin epidermis, and blood vessels close to the skin surface—hence the obvious appearance of redness. Sensitive skin is often the result of a defect in the skin's protective outer layer—known as the epidermal lipid barrier layer—allowing irritants, microbes and allergens to penetrate the skin and cause adverse reactions. A disturbed epidermal lipid barrier is an important component in several inflammatory skin diseases and disorders, such as rosacea, atopic dermatitis, psoriasis and eczema.

Rather than a result of genetics, sensitized skin is a reflection of your environment, lifestyle and physiology. Pollution, stress, hormonal fluctuations, smoking, alcohol, poor diet, medical procedures and even over-processed or exfoliated skin can all lead to sensitization. Cosmetic ingredients including alcohol, lanolin, fragrance and D&C colorants can also lead to sensitized skin. While those with fair skin (usually of Northern European ancestry) traditionally experience sensitive skin, sensitized skin can be triggered in any person regardless of racial background or skin color.

In addition to the factors presented by a hostile world, our own microclimate is also an important factor. The microclimate we expose our skin to in our homes, cars, offices and airplanes changes daily, resulting in varying levels of sensitivity. For instance, we may be inadvertently sensitizing our skin on a typical winter day, when we transfer from cold, dry winds outside to dry forced-air heating inside.

Regardless of the classification of skin sensitivity versus sensitization, the common thread among these conditions is inflammation.

Adapted from an article by Dr. Diana Howard.

SALON**CONNECTION**

What Role Does Skin Type Play in Salon Services?

Here are some examples from salon menus promoting services for different skin types.

>> *Essential Facial* – A custom facial for your individual needs and skin type. This analysis includes cleansing, toning, exfoliation with steam and a customized masque treatment. *Cathryn Jamieson Salon*

>> *Veranda Signature Facial* – Whether your skin is dry, environmentally damaged, sensitive, or oily, the Prescriptive Facial is appropriate for any skin type. From pharmaceutical-grade ingredients used in clinical treatments to luxurious indulgences, your skin will benefit from the correct facial treatment. *Veranda Salon • Massage • Medi-Spa*

>> *EFS Signature Facial* – Experience the calming and soothing Signature Facial, the ultimate skin care treatment. Included in this serene experience is deep pore cleansing by extraction, exfoliation, skin rebalancing and a gentle massage. This facial is recommended for all skin types. Each facial can be customized with one of our a la carte services based on your skin needs. *Eric Fisher Salon*

TYPES OF SKIN

Skin type is our genetic predisposition, which makes each person's skin different. It is the changes in our lifestyle, environment, illness or hormonal imbalances that will affect the general condition of the skin. If the skin is constantly neglected, side effects such as blemishes, wrinkles, flakiness, roughness and a general lack of healthy color may appear. The skin requires a certain amount of care and attention on a daily basis to stay healthy and attractive.

Although the structure of each person's skin is basically the same, the functioning of the various glands and the reactions of the skin to its environment can vary greatly. From a salon professional's point of view, the surface of the skin falls into four basic types:

>> Dry

>> Oily

>> Normal

>> Combination

It is important for you to recognize these four types so that the proper cleansing and moisturizing regimen can be recommended for each client.

As a salon professional, you'll be expected to provide skin care services that offer special attention for a wide variety of clients. Being sensitive to each client will ensure they return for the benefits of your care.

DRY SKIN

Dry skin is characterized by signs such as peeling and flaking. It chaps easily and has a general all-over taut feeling. Dry skin has fewer blemishes and is not prone to acne. There are two types of dry skin: oil dry and moisture dry.

>> Oil dry skin lacks sebaceous activity, while moisture dry skin lacks water.

>> Although dry skin is often associated with more mature skin, it can be found on a younger person, as well.

>> Dry skin can be caused by many factors, including a systemic malfunction of the sebaceous glands, diet, hormones or a combination of these conditions.

>> To keep your skin in its optimum condition, you should drink half your body weight in ounces of water per day.

>> A good treatment program is essential for dry skin to supply moisture, emollients and lubricants necessary for healthy, soft, smooth skin.

OILY SKIN

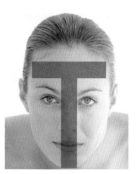

Oily skin usually has an all-over shiny look and/or a rough texture with blackheads and enlarged pores. The oily residue most often appears on the chin, nose, nasal-labial groove and forehead, which is commonly called the T-zone. In a young person, oily skin is prone to acne, but the cause of acne cannot be attributed solely to oily skin. Any combination of conditions may be responsible, such as improper cleansing, hormonal imbalance, nervous conditions, poor diet and even humid weather.

>> A good treatment program is important to keep oily skin pH-balanced (pH of 4.5-5.5). Avoid using harsh alkaline ingredients that would cause a stripping effect for this skin type.

>> Maintaining the skin's pH balance helps inhibit the invasion of pathogenic bacteria that can contribute to skin infection. It also maintains the skin in its "natural" environment, causing less irritation.

NORMAL SKIN

Normal skin is very rare. It is recognized by its fresh, healthy glow and color; firm, moist and smooth texture; no blackheads or blemishes; and does not appear oily.

>> This skin type requires a simple but consistent skin care routine to keep it in this condition.

>> The treatment objective for normal skin is to maintain its natural, acid-balanced condition.

COMBINATION SKIN

The most common skin type is combination skin. It can be found on people of most any age and is recognized by the shiny T-zone (forehead, nose, and chin) and the presence of a noticeable dryness in the cheek, jawline and hairline areas. Blackheads and enlarged pores are often evident on the nose and chin.

>> Combination skin requires the most specialized skin regimen, as you are treating two totally different skin types at the same time—oily and dry.

>> The treatment goal for this skin type is to stabilize the oily areas and lubricate the dry areas.

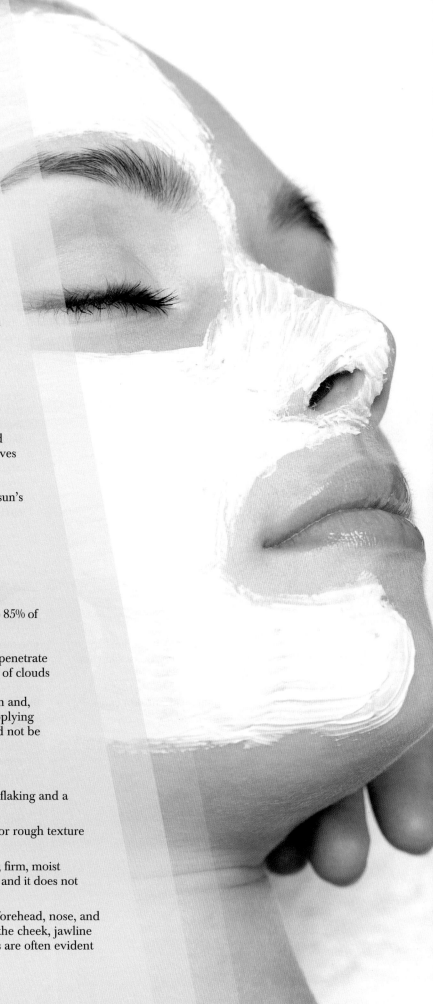

LESSONS LEARNED

The skin has six basic functions, which include:

>> Sensation – Makes you aware of heat, cold, touch, pain and pressure through nerve endings just under the outer layer of the skin

>> Heat regulation – Maintains our internal heat regardless of environmental climate

>> Absorption – Permits certain substances like water and oxygen to pass through tissues

>> Protection – Protects the body against blows and falls and direct impact of heat and cold

>> Excretion – Eliminates sweat, salt and wastes from the body

>> Secretion – Maintains a normal pH range of 4.5-5.5 through the use of sebum

The skin is composed of three main layers: The epidermis, known as the outermost, protective layer; the dermal layer, known as the living layer; and the subcutaneous layer, which is the fatty layer that gives contour and shape to the body.

Examples of how to protect the skin by reducing the sun's harmful effects include:

>> Applying a sunscreen with an SPF of at least 30, reapplying every 2 hours

>> Wearing protective, tightly woven clothing

>> Avoiding surfaces, such as water, that can reflect up to 85% of the sun's damaging rays

>> Knowing that damaging UVA and UVB rays can penetrate windows, car windshields, our clothing and layers of clouds

>> Protecting children by keeping them out of the sun and, beginning at 6 months of age, minimize risk by applying sunscreen; children younger than 6 months should not be exposed to the sun

The basic types of skin surfaces include:

>> Dry – Characterized by signs such as peeling and flaking and a general all-over taut feeling

>> Oily – Recognized by an all-over shiny look and/or rough texture with blackheads and enlarged pores

>> Normal – Recognized by a fresh and healthy color; firm, moist and smooth texture, no blackheads and blemishes; and it does not appear oily

>> Combination – Recognized by the shiny T-zone (forehead, nose, and chin) and the presence of a noticeable dryness in the cheek, jawline and hairline areas; blackheads and enlarged pores are often evident on the nose and chin

EXPLORE //

Have you ever
had your skin
break out—
right before a
special event?

SKIN DISEASES
AND DISORDERS | 112.2

INSPIRE //

Your clients will look to you to make recommendations related
to their skin care.

ACHIEVE //

Following this lesson on *Skin Diseases and Disorders*,
you'll be able to:

>> Identify primary and secondary lesions

>> Offer examples of pigmentation abnormalities

>> Describe disorders of the sebaceous and sudoriferous glands

>> Summarize common skin infections

FOCUS //

SKIN DISEASES
AND DISORDERS

Lesions

Pigmentation
Abnormalities

Disorders

Skin Infections

112.2 | SKIN DISEASES AND DISORDERS

As a professional, you need to be familiar with skin disorders and diseases so you can recognize any problems that would prevent you from performing a skin care service. Keep in mind that only a dermatologist or other medical doctor should diagnose and treat skin diseases and disorders. In this lesson, certain conditions are accompanied by an asterisk (*), which indicates that skin care services may not be performed on the affected area.

The **symptoms** or signs of a disease are divided into two classifications:

>> Subjective – Those that can be felt (by the individual)

>> Objective – Those that can be seen (by the individual and observers)

In other words, signs of a disorder or disease may be felt but may not be visible. For example: Itching, burning and pain are examples of subjective symptoms. Pimples, rashes and inflammation are objective symptoms because they are visible. In some cases, both objective and subjective symptoms may be present and can be indications of an infection.

There are six signs of infection: pain, swelling, redness, local fever (heat), throbbing and discharge. Always avoid performing services on skin where symptoms indicate an infection may be present. Avoid direct contact with open wounds and/or lesions.

Important Vocabulary

Common terms related to the study of diseases and disorders and their definitions include:

>> An **allergy** is a sensitivity that may develop from contact with normally harmless substances. Symptoms of an allergy may include itching, redness, swelling and/or blisters.

>> **Inflammation** is an objective symptom characterized by redness, pain, swelling and/or increased temperature.

>> **Chronic** is a term used to identify conditions that are frequent and habitual.

>> **Acute** is a term used to identify conditions that are brief and severe.

>> A **contagious disease** is communicable by contact. It is also known as an infectious or communicable disease.

>> **Seasonal disease** is influenced by weather.

>> **Etiology** is the study of the causes of diseases.

>> **Pathology** is the study of diseases.

DISCOVER**MORE**

Eyes On Cancer

Eyes on Cancer.org is a nonprofit cancer awareness organization that teaches beauty professionals to identify early stage skin cancer. The organization is committed to seeing cancer stop hurting people both through cancer awareness and research for the cure for skin cancer. The Eyes On Cancer goal is to reduce cancer fatality rates by leveraging those first-line responders that are naturally in a position to spot skin cancer/melanoma at its earliest stages. Their philosophy is "trained eyes save lives."

The ABCDEs of Skin Cancer

Train your eyes to see the changes in the skin that suggest the need for physician evaluation. Statistically speaking, most melanomas start from a mole or center, spreading into the surrounding, normal skin. This superficial spread is its earliest stage when removal can be curative. Any one of the following suggests spread and requires physician evaluation:

A Asymmetry – Asymmetrical, or inconsistent growths; refer to a physician.

B Border – Has a well-defined edge and does not "bleed," (meaning blend or fade) into the surrounding skin.

C Color – Consistent; does not vary within growth.

D Diameter – Should be no larger than an eraser head on a pencil.

E Evolution – Increasing size (take a picture).

If it grows, bleeds or bothers, have it checked.

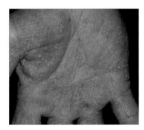

Occupational disorders occur in certain types of employment. For example, salon professionals may be susceptible to **dermatitis venenata** (dur-mah-**TYE**-tis ven-eh-**NAY**-tah), sometimes referred to as contact dermatitis. Contact dermatitis is a condition in which the skin becomes red, sore or inflamed after direct contact with a substance. There are two kinds of contact dermatitis: Irritant or allergic.

>> **Irritant contact dermatitis** is the most common type. It is caused by contact with acids, alkaline materials such as soaps and detergents, solvents or other chemicals such as hair dyes or perm solutions. The reaction usually looks like a burn and often shows as dry, red and rough skin.

>> **Allergic contact dermatitis** is caused by exposure to substances or materials such as fragrances, cosmetics, soaps, hair dyes, perm solutions, nail polish or latex gloves to which a person has become extra-sensitive or allergic and often causes a red, streaky or patchy rash where the substance touched the skin. The allergic reaction is often delayed, with the rash appearing 24-48 hours after exposure. Hands that are immersed in water and shampoo many times a day are at high risk. Protective creams are available to provide a barrier for the skin. Infection control practices establish standards regarding protective gloves, goggles, surgical masks, etc., to assist in avoiding occupational disorders.

LESIONS

Diseases and disorders are often accompanied by skin lesions, which are abnormal changes in the structure of an organ or tissue. There are three categories of lesions: Primary, Secondary and Tertiary.

PRIMARY SKIN LESIONS

Primary skin lesions are changes in the structure of the skin during the early stages of change and development.

PRIMARY SKIN LESIONS			
Macules	Freckles Lentigo		**Discoloration appearing on the skin's surface** » Flat areas and, although they are usually rounded and distinct, they may be oval, irregular or have an outline that gradually fades into surrounding tissues. Freckles commonly found on the face, neck and chest, are considered macules. A lentigo, which appears larger and darker than a freckle, is also an example of a macule. The plural form of lentigo is lentigines.
Vesicles*	**Bulla*** **Herpes Simplex***		**Fluid-filled elevations in the skin caused by localized accumulation of fluids or blood just below the epidermis** » May develop from macules, papules or poison oak or ivy and are generally short-lived. **Bulla** are lesions, like vesicles, but larger. Found above and below the skin, they contain a clear, watery fluid. They occur in cases of second-degree burns. **Herpes Simplex Virus** is a contagious, chronic condition characterized by a single vesicle or a group of vesicles on a red, swollen base. » Herpes Simplex Virus 1 (HSV-1), also called fever blisters or cold sores, usually appears on the lips, nostrils or other parts of the face. » Herpes Simplex Virus 2 (HSV-2) affects the genital region.
Papules	Tubercle Pimple		**Hardened red elevations of the skin in which no fluid is present** » Normally vary in size from that of a pinhead to that of a pea. The actual shape and coloration of the lesions may also vary. » Consistency may vary from hard to soft. » Papules may persist unchanged but they can sometimes proceed to other types of primary lesions. A large papule is known as a tubercle. A pimple is an example of a papule.
Pustules*	Pimple With Pus		**Small elevations of skin similar to vesicles in size and shape, but containing pus** » Appear whitish or yellowish in color and may be surrounded by a reddish inflammatory border. » May develop from vesicles or papules. A pimple with pus is an example of a pustule.
Wheals	Hives*		**Solid formation above the skin, often caused by an insect bite or allergic reaction** » Sharply defined and solid, rising above the skin (e.g., a mosquito bite). » Usually develop rapidly, disappear slowly and are accompanied by itching or tingling. Hives*, also called urticaria (ur-ti-**KAR**-e-uh), are examples of wheal lesions.
Tumors*	**Nodule** **Cyst** (sist)		**Solid masses in the skin, may be elevated or deep** » Usually more than one centimeter in diameter. » May be soft or hard, depending upon their makeup, and may be fixed or freely movable. » Classification often includes any new skin growths and any localized swelling, which generally have rounded shape. A **nodule** is a small tumor. A **cyst** is an abnormal membranous sac containing a gaseous, liquid or semi-solid substance.

*Indicates that services may not be performed on the affected area.

SECONDARY SKIN LESIONS

Secondary skin lesions appear as a disease progresses into the later stages of development.

SECONDARY SKIN LESIONS

Scales		**Shedding, dead cells of the uppermost layer of the epidermis** » Epidermis normally undergoes constant exfoliation (removal) of small, barely perceptible flakes of skin. » When the formation of epidermal cells is rapid or the normal process of keratinization is altered, abnormal exfoliation of the epidermis occurs, which results in scales. » Scales may be dry, such as psoriasis, or oily, such as dandruff. **Round, dry patches of skin, covered with rough, silvery scales** » It is chronic and not contagious. » Service unless skin is inflamed or broken in the area to be serviced.
	Psoriasis* (soh-**RYE**-ah-sis)	
Crusts*		**Dried masses that are the remains of an oozing sore** » Crusty material may contain blood, pus, sebum, epithelial tissue and/or bacterial debris. The scab on a sore is an example of a crust.
	Scab	
Excoriations*		**Mechanical abrasions to the epidermis or injuries to the epidermis** » Appear bright to dark red, because of dried blood, and occur when an insect bite or a scab is scratched. Scratches to the surface of the skin are considered excoriations.
Fissures*		**Cracks in the skin** » Usually appear as cracks or lines that may go as deep as the underlying dermal layer. May be dry or moist. » Often occur when skin loses its flexibility due to exposure to wind, cold, water, etc. Chapped lips are one example of a fissure.
Scars	Cicatrix (**SIK**-uh-triks) Keloids	**Formations resulting from a lesion** » Extend into the dermal layer or deeper, as part of the normal healing process. » Scars are permanent; however, they generally become less noticeable with time. The size and shape of a scar are dependent upon the extent of the original injury. Keloids are thick scars.
Ulcers*		**Open lesions** » May result in the loss of portions of the dermal layer. » May be accompanied by pus.

*Indicates that services may not be performed on the affected area.

As a salon professional, you need to recognize primary and secondary lesions.

Hypertrophy is a skin classification that identifies common skin conditions that involve an overgrowth or excess of skin (new growth).

HYPERTROPHIES	
Callus	Sometimes called **hyperkeratosis** or **keratoma**, is a **thickening of the epidermis** ›› An example is a corn, which occurs from pressure and friction applied to the skin.
Verruca*	**Name given to a variety of warts** ›› Warts are caused by a virus, can be contagious, and can spread all over the body. ›› A dermatologist or other medical doctor should be consulted for removal of warts. ›› Warts are referred to as the most common tumor.
Skin Tags	**Small, elevated growths of skin** ›› Small benign nodule, which can easily be removed by a physician.
	*Indicates that services may not be performed on the affected area.

PIGMENTATION ABNORMALITIES

Pigmentation abnormalities describe conditions of too much color or too little color in a particular area of the skin. Two types, Melanodermas and Leukodermas, are presented here.

Melanoderma is the term used to describe any **hyperpigmentation** caused by overactivity of the melanocytes in the epidermis. It can be triggered by overexposure to sunlight, overactivity of the pituitary gland, circulation of hormones, disease and drugs. Examples of melanoderma include chloasma, moles and nevus.

Chloasma	(kloh-**AZ**-mah)	**Group of brownish macules (nonelevated spots) occurring in one place** ›› Chloasma is commonly called liver spots and often occurs on the hands and face.
Moles		**Small, brown pigmented spots that may be raised** ›› Hair often grows through moles, but should not be removed, unless advised by a physician. ›› If there is any change in appearance of a mole, seek medical advice.
	Melanotic Sarcoma	Melanotic sarcoma is a skin cancer that begins with a mole.
Nevus	(**NEE**-vus)	**Birthmark or a congenital mole** ›› A birthmark may look like a stain on the face or other part of the body and is generally a reddish purple flat mark. ›› The stain is caused by dilation of the small blood vessels in the skin.

Leukoderma (loo-ko-**DUR**-mah) describes **hypopigmentation** (lack of pigmentation) of the skin caused by a decrease in activity of melanocytes. Leukoderma is occasionally the result of a congenital defect such as albinism, or can be acquired, as in vitiligo.

Albinism 	(**AL**-bin-izm)	**Congenital failure of the skin to produce melanin pigment** » Persons with albinism have pink skin, white hair (it may sometimes be reddish) and pink eyes. They have a strong hypersensitivity to light and sun and their skin ages early. » This skin should be protected from exposure to sunlight and ultraviolet lamps.
Vitiligo	(vit-i-**LYE**-goh)	**Characterized by oval or irregular patches of white skin that do not have normal pigment** » Vitiligo is usually seen on the face, hands and neck as patches of hypopigmentation that may enlarge slowly. » These patches of skin must be protected from exposure to sunlight or ultraviolet lamps.

DISORDERS

DISORDERS OF THE SEBACEOUS GLANDS

Comedones (**KOM**-e-donz), are small bumps frequently found on the forehead and chin associated with acne. Open comedones are blackheads–black because of surface pigment (melanin) versus dirt. Closed comedones are whiteheads–the follicle is completely blocked. Comedones can be removed with proper extraction procedures.

Milia (**MIL**-ee-uh), are pearly white, enclosed keratin-filled cysts that contain sebum, dead skin cells and bacteria which form a hard ball beneath the outer layer of the skin.

Acne (**AK**-nee) is a genetic disease that occurs most often on the face, back and chest and is a chronic, inflammatory disorder of the sebaceous glands. Dead skin cells and sebum collect at the base of the hair follicle and block the flow of oxygen allowing bacteria to multiply. It is most often accompanied by lesions such as pimples, pustules and cysts.

Rosacea* (ro-**ZAY**-sha), or acne rosacea, is a chronic inflammatory congestion of the cheeks and nose, observed as redness, with papules and sometimes pustules present. Advise clients to avoid excessive heat, spicy foods and caffeine. Facials may be done under physician's approval.

Asteatosis (as-tee-ah-**TOH**-sis) is a condition of dry, scaly skin with reduced sebum production.

Seborrheic dermatitis (seb-oh-**REE**-ick) (a form of eczema) is a common skin rash with redness and scaly, pinkish-yellow patches that have an oily appearance. It usually affects the scalp.

Steatoma (stee-ah-**TOH**-mah), or sebaceous cyst or wen, is a subcutaneous tumor of the sebaceous gland, filled with sebum. This disorder usually appears on the scalp, neck or back and ranges in size from a pea to an orange.

Furuncles* (fu-**RUN**-kels), or boils, appear in the dermal layer and the epidermis and are caused by an acute bacterial infection. They are localized infections of hair follicles. Carbuncles* refers to a cluster of furuncles and are caused by an acute bacterial infection of several adjoining hair follicles.

*Indicates that services may not be performed on the affected area.

DISORDERS OF THE SUDORIFEROUS GLANDS

Bromidrosis (broh-mih-**DROH**-sis) (body odor) is a medical condition characterized by an unpleasant odor from the skin.

Anhidrosis (an-heye-**DROH**-sis) is the inability to sweat normally. Overexposure to the sun or a high fever due to illness can lead to serious illness or heat stroke.

Hyperhidrosis (hy-per-hy-**DROH**-sis) is an over-production of perspiration caused by excessive heat or general body weakness and requires medical attention.

Miliaria rubra* (mil-ee-**AY**-re-ah **ROOB**-rah), or prickly heat, is an acute eruption of small red vesicles with burning and itching of the skin caused by excessive heat.

*Indicates that services may not be performed on the affected area.

SKIN INFECTIONS

Common skin infections include:

>> **Dermatitis*** (dur-mah-**TYE**-tis) is an inflammatory infection of the skin.

>> **Eczema*** (**EK**-sah-mah) is characterized by dry or moist lesions with inflammation of the skin. Eczema may be chronic or acute and should be referred to a physician for treatment.

>> **Impetigo*** (im-peh-**TIE**-go) is a highly contagious bacterial infection that produces a honey-yellow, crusted lesion, usually on the face.

>> **Folliculitis*** (fo-lik-u-**LYE**-tis) is an infection in the hair follicles caused by bacteria, shaving or clothing irritation. It usually looks like a red pimple with a hair in the center.

>> **Pseudofolliculitis barbae*** (**SOO**-doh-fo-lik-u-li-tis **BAR**-be) is the medical term for razor bumps or irritation following shaving.

>> **Conjunctivitis*** (kuhn-juhngk-tuh-**VYE**-tis), referred to as pink eye, is an inflammation of the transparent membrane that lines the eyelid and eyeball; characterized by itching and redness; spreads easily.

*Indicates that services may not be performed on the affected area.

Tinea (**TIN**-ee-ah) is the medical term for ringworm. It is a contagious fungal disease characterized by a red circular patch of blisters, caused by a fungal vegetable parasite. These fungi have the ability to infect the outermost cornified layers of the skin, hair or nails. Humidity and moisture provide a favorable environment for the fungi, making infections more common in skin folds, the groin or between the toes. These infections are classified according to location:

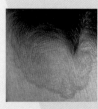

Tinea corporis

>> Tinea capitis – Scalp

>> Tinea faciei – Face

>> Tinea corporis – Trunk and extremities

>> Tinea cruris – Groin

>> Tinea manuum and tinea pedis – Hands and feet

>> Tinea unguium or onychomycosis – Nails

Your ability to identify skin diseases and disorders will allow you to confidently make recommendations for your clients' skin care needs.

LESSONS LEARNED

Primary skin lesions are changes in the structure of the skin during the early stages of change and development. Primary skin lesions include: Macules, vesicles*, papules, pustules*, wheals and tumors*.

Secondary skin lesions appear as a disease progresses into the later stages of development. Secondary skin lesions include: scales, psoriasis*, crusts*, excoriations*, fissures*, scars and ulcers*.

Hypertrophies identify overgrowth or excess of skin with examples including callus, verruca* and skin tags.

Pigmentation abnormalities describe conditions of too much color or too little color in a particular area of the skin and consist of two types: Melanoderma (chloasma, moles, naevus) and leukoderma (albinism, vitiligo).

Disorders of the sebaceous glands include:

>> Comedones – Open (blackhead); Closed (whitehead)

>> Milia – Keratin-filled cyst

>> Acne – Pimples, pustules and cysts

>> Rosacea* – Redness with papules and sometimes pustules on the cheeks and nose

>> Asteatosis – Dry, scaly skin with reduced sebum production

>> Seborrheic Dermatitis – Skin rash

>> Steatoma – Sebaceous cyst or wen; subcutaneous tumor of the sebaceous gland, filled with sebum

>> Furuncles* – Boils; acute bacterial infection

Disorders of the sudoriferous glands include:

>> Bromidrosis – Body odor

>> Anhidrosis – Inability to sweat normally

>> Hyperhidrosis – Overproduction of perspiration

>> Miliaria rubra* – Acute eruption of small red vesicles with burning and itching of the skin caused by excessive heat

A summary of common skin infections includes:

>> Dermatitis* – An inflammatory disorder of the skin

>> Eczema* – Characterized by dry or moist lesions with inflammation of the skin

>> Impetigo*– Highly contagious bacterial infection that produces a honey-yellow, crusted lesion, usually on the face

>> Folliculitis* – Infection in the hair follicles caused by bacteria, shaving or clothing irritation

>> Pseudofolliculitis barbae* – Medical term for razor bumps or irritation following shaving

>> Conjunctivitis*– Pink eye; an inflammation of the transparent membrane that lines the eyelid and eyeball; characterized by itching and redness; spreads easily

>> Tinea – Medical term for ringworm

*Indicates that services may not be performed on the affected area.

SKIN CARE 112.3

What do you currently do to take care of your skin?

INSPIRE //

Helping clients establish a skin care regimen and feel the benefits of massage will enhance their well-being and expand your career horizons.

ACHIEVE //

Following this lesson on *Skin Care*, you'll be able to:

>> Identify the skin care regimen recommended for healthy skin

>> State the benefits of each of the five types of massage movements used during facial massage

>> Describe the types of common facial masks used for skin care

FOCUS //

SKIN CARE
Skin Care Regimen
Massage
Facial Masks

Proper skin care is a combination of concerted efforts toward a good home-maintenance program, a well-balanced diet, proper intake of water, limited exposure to the sun, exercise, rest and professional skin care treatments and products.

SKIN CARE REGIMEN

Keeping the skin in good condition requires a regimen of skin care. There are four steps that are recommended daily to ensure healthy skin: cleanse, tone, moisturize and protect.

Cleanse thoroughly with a product that does not rob or strip the skin of its natural conditioners.

>> The skin should be cleansed daily with an appropriate skin-cleaning product.

>> Ordinary soaps are not recommended for cleansing since they are generally alkaline and can strip the skin of its protective acid mantle.

Tone the skin with a water-based product called a toner that contains beneficial ingredients, such as skin-repairing substances and antioxidants.

>> Using toners helps to further cleanse, soothe and smooth the skin while bringing it to a normal pH.

Moisturize the skin to make up for the unavoidable losses it sustains from aging and exposure to the environment.

>> Helps to keep the skin smooth.

>> Moisturizers in a product operate in several ways. Some products, called humectants, attract moisture. Other products create a barrier that helps keep moisture in.

>> It is important to remember that oily skin needs moisturizing (hydrating) as much as dry skin. Excessive oil in skin does not replace loss of moisture. In fact, proper moisturizing can actually reduce the oily appearance because it contributes to a better balance of oil and moisture in the skin.

Protect the skin from the damaging effects of sun exposure by wearing sunscreen.

>> The purpose of sunscreen is to protect the skin from the harmful UVA and UVB rays projected from the sun.

>> Remember to include lip balm with an SPF (Sun Protection Factor) of at least 30 if you are going to be active outdoors.

Toners fall into three categories, which include:

1. **Water-based formulas**

>> Contain beneficial ingredients, such as skin-repairing substances and antioxidants

>> Recommended for skin care to help bring skin to a normal pH following the use of a cleanser

2. **Alcohol-based formulas**

>> Often include "astringent" ingredients, such as witch hazel

>> Toners with alcohol and astringent ingredients may cause irritation to the skin

3. **Water and glycerin or glycol-based formulas with fragrant extracts**

>> Contain ingredients, such as rose water or citrus fruit

>> Often are labeled as fresheners or clarifiers

DISCOVER**MORE**

While many believe exfoliation to be a relatively new trend in skin care, the reality could not be further from the truth. History overflows with anecdotes of exfoliation practices. For example, Cleopatra took frequent milk baths to maintain her complexion. Little did she know, her positive results were due to the milk's lactic acid content, which gently exfoliated her skin. In ancient Egypt, they applied wine to the skin, of which the tartaric acid content helped to minimize the signs of aging. The ancient Greeks and Romans applied a mix of pumice and oils to their skin, which allowed them to mechanically exfoliate.

In more modern days, dermatologists began using chemicals to minimize the signs of aging in the late 1800s. By the 1970s, dermabrasion was introduced as a professional treatment. The selection of properly formulated home-care exfoliation products was limited, however, to harsh facial scrubs until the early 1990s when alpha hydroxy acids entered the market by way of moisturizers. It is that singular development that dramatically changed the skin care industry. Today, alpha hydroxy acids are found in nearly all skin care product categories, with a vast selection of exfoliation products available for homecare use. Many of these exfoliants provide excellent results that complement professional treatments and, in some cases, even rival them.

Excerpted from Dermascope.com
Abdullah, M.D., F.A.C.S., F.I.C.S.

EXFOLIATION

As we age, cell turnover in adults will slow down from every 30 to 45 days in our 20s and 30s, to as much as 45 to 60 days every decade or so, giving the skin a sluggish and unhealthy appearance. The role of **exfoliation** is to remove the outer layer of epidermal cells, revealing newer skin beneath. This shedding of the outer layer helps unclog pores, aids in reducing acne breakouts, encourages cell renewal and promotes optimum skin fitness and health.

The two main ways of exfoliating the skin are either mechanical (physical) or chemical.

>> **Mechanical exfoliation** is the superficial loosening and reduction of cells in the outer-most layer of the epidermis. This would include methods such as facial cloths, scrubs or a brush. This is also called manual exfoliation.

>> **Chemical exfoliation** is the process of using natural substances such as enzymes or hydroxy acids in conjunction with other ingredients to cause a chemical reaction to remove dead skin cells. Different chemical agents promote rapid cell turnover, depending on how deeply they penetrate the layers of the skin. Exfoliants leave the skin smooth, soft and more receptive to the beneficial products applied directly afterward. Proper skin exfoliation, especially of the entire body, enhances nerve stimulation and skin respiration.

Regardless of type or method, an exfoliant applied at least once a week should mimic the skin's natural processes, like the enzymes that help promote and increase cell turnover.

In addition to cleansing, toning, moisturizing and protection, getting regular professional facial services, such as a basic facial, helps keep your clients' skin in optimum condition. Two of the steps generally performed in a facial include massage and facial masks.

MASSAGE

Massage dates back to the ancient Greeks, who used it as a cure for ailments. Women had their bodies massaged with vegetable and animal oils to keep their skin soft. Massage is a systematic, therapeutic method of manipulating the body by rubbing, pinching, tapping, kneading or stroking with the hands, fingers or an instrument.

Massage is an excellent method for providing a restful, relaxing skin care treatment to a client. Every muscle and nerve has a motor point. Applying pressure to motor points soothes and stimulates the nerves and muscles (see illustration). There are many additional benefits of massage:

1. Increases circulation of the blood supply to the skin, causing blood vessels to dilate

2. Contracts the muscle when the movement is firm and rapid

3. Stimulates the glandular activities of the skin

4. Strengthens weak muscle tissue; relieves pain

5. Softens and improves the texture and complexion of the skin

6. Calms and relaxes the client and can relieve emotional stress and body tension

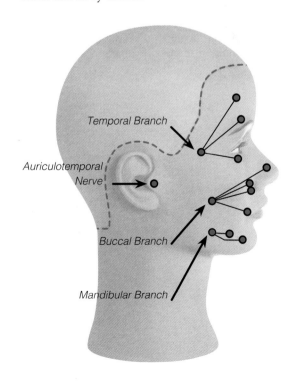

Temporal Branch

Auriculotemporal Nerve

Buccal Branch

Mandibular Branch

DISCOVERMORE

One cigarette depletes the body of 15 mg to 25 mg of vitamin C. A vitamin C deficiency can contribute to cellular breakdown. Long-term effects will speed up the aging and wrinkling process. Also, ingesting large amounts of caffeine, such as in coffee, tea or soft drinks, will affect not only the appearance but also the internal functioning of the skin. Research indicates that drinking a large amount of caffeine over a period of time will contribute to cellular aging.

Drinking a lot of alcohol leaves the skin dehydrated. Alcohol steals the good hydration and leaves the bad, which results in dryness, bloating and redness. Drinking water is the only way to combat the drying effects of alcohol.

Alcohol can also affect conditions like rosacea, causing it to get worse or become more acute. Alcohol increases blood flow, which can cause blood vessels in your face to dilate and sometimes burst, leaving behind broken capillaries and red spots that are difficult to get rid of. Even if you have a few drinks a week, it is important to understand how the alcohol may be affecting your skin.

CONTRAINDICATIONS FOR MASSAGE

Contraindications (conditions or factors that serve as reasons to withhold certain treatments) to consider before performing a massage service are presented in the following chart.

MEDICAL CONDITIONS	REASONS
Pregnancy	General safety precaution; be guided by physician permission
Heart conditions/pacemaker, high blood pressure	Heart rhythms and pacemakers can be affected by electrical treatment; massage increases circulation and could present a risk for clients with high blood pressure or a prior stroke
Sensitive, redness-prone skin	Redness could intensify; avoid heat, harsh scrubs, stimulating massage, mechanical treatment
Metal bone pins or plates	Metal can be affected by electrical treatment
Known allergies	Occurrence of allergic reaction; avoid using known allergens or fragrances
Autoimmune diseases such as lupus	General safety precaution; intense treatments require physician's permission
Diabetes	General safety precaution; intense treatments require physician's permission
Open sores, herpes simplex virus 1 and 2	Can spread; avoid all treatments; physician's permission required
Recent facial surgery or laser treatment	Safety precaution; physician's permission required

CERTAIN MEDICATIONS	
Accutane, exfoliating medications such as Retin-A®, Renova®, Tazorac®, Differin®; Certain antibiotics for acne treatment	Can cause skin to blister or peel; avoid peeling/drying agents such as alpha hydroxy acids (AHAs), scrubs, microdermabrasion and brushing machines
Blood thinners	May cause bleeding or bruising; require physician's permission
Oral steroids	Can cause thinning of the skin that leads to blistering or injury; avoid any stimulating or exfoliating treatment

In most areas, salon professionals may massage the head, face, neck, shoulders, upper back, hands, arms and feet. For a complete body massage, you may be required to refer your client to a licensed massage therapist. Refer to your area's regulatory agency for massage therapy licensure requirements.

THE 5 BASIC MOVEMENTS OF MASSAGE

	EFFLEURAGE (EF-loo-rahzh)	A light, gliding, gentle stroking or circular movement. It is used on the face, neck and arms, and is often used as the movement that begins and ends a massage treatment. This method is carried out with the palms of the hands or with the pads of the fingertips. The beneficial effect of effleurage is that it is relaxing and soothing.
	PETRISSAGE (PAY-tre-sahzh)	A light or heavy kneading and rolling of the muscles. It is used on the face, the arms, the shoulders and the upper back. Petrissage is probably the most important of the massage movements due to its beneficial effects. It is done by kneading the muscles between the thumb and fingers or by pressing the palm of the hand firmly over the muscles, then grasping and squeezing with the heel of the hand and the fingers. The beneficial effects of petrissage are deep stimulation of muscles, nerves and skin glands; promotes the circulation of blood and lymph.
	TAPOTEMENT (tah-POHT-mant)	Percussion, or hacking, is a light tapping or slapping movement applied with the fingertips or partly flexed fingers. The movement is usually carried out with the hands swinging freely from the wrist in a rapid motion. It should not be used when the client needs soothing. Hacking is a form of tapotement that is similar to a chopping movement with the edge of the hands used on the arms, back and shoulders. The beneficial effects of tapotement include stimulating nerves, promoting muscle contraction and increasing blood circulation.
	FRICTION	A circular, or wringing movement with no gliding, usually carried out with the fingertips or palms of the hands. Friction is used most often on the scalp, hands or with less pressure during a facial massage. The beneficial effects of friction include stimulating nerves and increasing blood circulation.
	VIBRATION	A shaking movement in the arms of the salon professional, while the fingertips or palms are touching the client. Vibration should only be used in facial massage for a few seconds in one location, as it is very stimulating to the skin. The beneficial effect of vibration is that it is highly stimulating.

While performing the massage keep in mind:

>> **Massage should never be performed over an area exhibiting redness, swelling, pus, disease, bruises and/or broken or scraped skin.**

>> **Massage movements should be directed toward the origin of the muscles in order to avoid damage to muscle tissues.**

>> **When performing facial massage, an even tempo or rhythm is essential for the relaxation of the client.** Do not remove the hands from the face once the massage has begun and, if it becomes necessary, feather the hands off the face and gently replace them on the skin with the same feather-like movements.

FACIAL MASKS

Facial masks (or packs) are used for many different reasons including:
>> Cleansing
>> Hydration
>> Tightening of the pores
>> Exfoliation
>> Reduction of excess oil
>> Nourishment

Facial masks can be used in conjunction with facial services or they can be offered as a separate service. Facial masks are either applied directly to the skin or over a layer of gauze.

TYPES OF FACIAL MASKS

This chart identifies common masks with a brief description for each one.

MASKS	DESCRIPTION
Clay/Mud	>> Usually recommended for normal and oily skin types >> Leave an exfoliating effect by making large pores temporarily appear smaller
Cream	>> Recommended for normal to dry skin >> Result in moisturized skin
Gel	>> Designed for dry skin types and sensitive skin >> Many contain botanicals and ingredients designed to calm and soothe sensitive skin >> Make the skin look more supple and pliable
Modeling	>> Used for normal and oily skin >> Mixed with water and applied in a thick consistency to the face >> Dries and hardens to a rubber-like consistency within minutes, then can be pulled from the face in one piece >> Delivers the benefits of the ingredients from which they are made plus seals the skin, locking in moisture and creating a firm, taut feeling
Paraffin (Warm Wax)	>> Used for normal and dry skin >> Heated and applied to the skin to rehydrate (moisturize) the skin's top layers >> By coating the skin with warmth and blocking the skin's natural tendency to "breathe," the heat of the warm wax draws oil and perspiration to the top layer of the skin >> Especially good for dry, wrinkled or dehydrated skin >> Applied over a layer of gauze

The Benefits of Facial Masks

1. Increase skin's firmness temporarily

2. Increase blood circulation in the areas treated

3. Absorb and remove unwanted surface oil

4. Remove surface dirt

5. Absorb and remove skin impurities

6. Soften and smooth skin

7. Relax and refresh client

Being able to treat the skin in ways that encourage its healthy growth and appearance is a rewarding practice. If you excel at facials that relax and rejuvenate clients, as well as cleanse, tone, moisturize and protect the skin, you'll develop a loyal clientele.

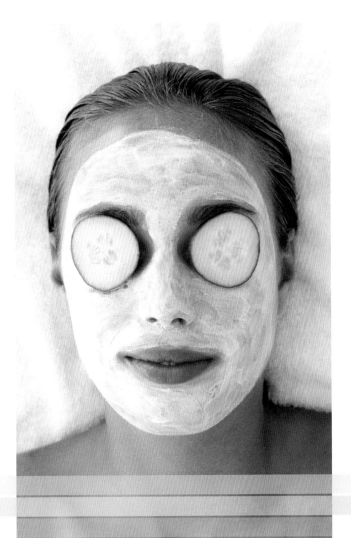

LESSONS LEARNED

The skin care regimen recommended for healthy skin is:

» *Cleanse* thoroughly with a product that does not rob or strip the skin of its natural conditioners.

» *Tone* the skin with a water-based product called a toner that contains beneficial ingredients such as skin-repairing substances and antioxidants.

» *Moisturize* the skin to make up for the unavoidable losses it sustains from aging and exposure to the environment.

» *Protect* the skin from the damaging effects of sun exposure.

» The benefits of each of the five types of massage movements used during facial massage are:

   ■ Effleurage – Relaxing and soothing

   ■ Petrissage – Deep stimulation of muscles, nerves and skin glands; promotes the circulation of blood and lymph

   ■ Tapotement – Stimulates nerves, promotes muscle contraction and increases blood circulation

   ■ Friction – Stimulates nerves and increases blood circulation

   ■ Vibration – Highly stimulating

The types of common facial masks used for skin care are:

» Clay/mud for normal and oily skin

» Cream for normal to dry skin

» Gel for dry skin types and sensitive skin

» Modeling for normal and oily skin

» Paraffin for normal and dry skin

112.4
SKIN CARE
GUEST EXPERIENCE

How would you describe the feeling of being pampered?

INSPIRE //

Giving clients the self-assurance that comes with beautiful, healthy skin is very rewarding.

ACHIEVE //

Following this lesson on *Skin Care Guest Experience,* you'll be able to:

>> Identify the service essentials related to skin care

>> Provide examples of infection control and safety guidelines for skin care services

>> Define the products used for skin care services

>> Explain the three areas of a basic facial service

FOCUS //

SKIN CARE GUEST EXPERIENCE

Skin Care Service Essentials

Skin Care Infection Control and Safety

Basic Facial Service Overview

Basic Facial Rubric

112.4 | SKIN CARE GUEST EXPERIENCE

It could be said that skin care is all about pampering. What exactly does pampering mean? Pampering means to give someone special treatment and to make them feel as comfortable as possible. It's all about indulgence. For example, think of the last time you experienced pampering. Were you on vacation or lying down to sleep in new bedding that was soft and lush? Did you get a VIP table at a restaurant, or did someone do something extra-special for you that you never expected?

For the salon guest, the skin care service can provide pampering at its best. It's an opportunity to not only tap into the client's feelings but to also offer healthy, glowing skin as a result.

SKIN CARE SERVICE ESSENTIALS

As with all professional services, consulting with your client prior to the actual service will ensure predictable results and will help you avoid any misunderstandings. As you review the four Service Essentials (four Cs), remember the importance of active listening, critical thinking and analysis on the overall success of the service.

SKIN CARE RECORD

Name_____ Phone Number_____
Address_____ City, State, Postal Code_____
Phone (H)_____ (C)_____
Occupation_____ Referred By_____

MEDICAL HISTORY
Age_____ Sex Female/Male
Known Allergies_____
Are you under the care of a Dermatologist?_____
Have you experienced any skin problems for the past 5 years?_____
If yes, please describe_____
Do you have any medical conditions such as:
High Blood Pressure_____ Heart Problems_____ Diabetes_____
Pregnancy_____ Pacemaker/metal implants_____
Are you on medication?_____
Other not listed above_____

DIETARY HISTORY
Are you currently dieting?_____
Do take supplements, vitamins, etc?_____
Do you exercise regularly?_____
Do you eat well-balanced meals?_____
Do you drink at least 8 glasses of water daily?_____

COSMETIC HISTORY
What is the purpose of this makeup appointment Day / Evening / Bridal
Have you ever had a reaction from skin care products or makeup products? Yes No
Explain_____
Cosmetics now being used_____
Extent of facial care at home:
Daily_____
Weekly_____

SKIN EVALUATION

SKIN TYPE	CHARACTERISTICS	SKIN CONDITION/ELASTICITY
Normal_____	White Heads_____	Normal_____
Dry_____	Comedones_____	Fair_____
Oily_____	Broken Capillaries_____	Poor_____
Combination_____	Discoloration_____	
_____	Blemishes_____	

SIGNS OF DEHYDRATION
None_____
Moderate_____   Acne_____   How long?_____
Severe_____   Juvenile_____   Vulgaris_____
Asphyxiated_____   Chronic_____   Cystic_____
(Blocked pores/Follicles) Rosacea_____ Scars_____
Wrinkles_____   Remarks_____

PRODUCT & TREATMENT RECOMMENDATIONS
Series Recommended: Corrective / Maintenance
Length of Time: (# of Weeks) 3 6 8 12

TREATMENT DATE	PROCEDURE	ESTHETICIAN

REMARKS_____

CONNECT

>> Meet and greet the client with a firm handshake and a pleasant tone of voice.

>> Communicate to build rapport and develop a relationship with the client.

>> Fill out a skin care record form with client (example provided at left).

CONSULT

>> Ask questions to discover client needs.

>> Analyze client's face and complete appropriate sections of the skin evaluation form (example provided at left).

>> Assess the facts and thoroughly think through your recommendations after reading the completed skin care record form.

>> Explain your recommended solutions, the products that will be used and the price of the service: Think not only of today's service but also future services.

>> Gain feedback and consent from your client.

>> Fill out the appropriate section(s) of the skin evaluation form to record your treatment plan.

CREATE

>> Protect client by practicing infection control procedures throughout the service.

>> Ensure client comfort during service.

>> Stay focused on delivering the service to the best of your ability.

>> Explain to your client the products you are using throughout the service and why.

>> Teach the client how to perform a home skin-care regimen.

COMPLETE

>> Request satisfaction feedback from your client.

>> Escort client to retail area, and recommend products to maintain appearance and condition of your client's skin.

>> Inform client that you keep these products in stock for purchase at all times.

>> Invite your client to make a purchase.

>> Ask your client for referrals for future services.

>> Suggest a future appointment time, and offer to prebook your client's next visit.

>> Offer appreciation to your client for visiting the school or salon.

>> Discard single-use items, and clean and disinfect multi-use supplies.

>> Record recommended products on client record for future visits.

COMMUNICATION GUIDELINES

Respond to common client cues in a way that encourages client trust and open communication.

CLIENT CUE	SALON PROFESSIONAL RESPONSE
"My skin feels very dry; I can't seem to use enough moisturizer, yet I keep breaking out along the sides of my chin."	"Judging from the look of your skin and what you are telling me, it seems as though your oil glands are producing plenty of oil, causing some breakouts. Your skin is probably not dry, but dehydrated, which creates that 'dry' feeling. My recommendation is to begin today with an enzyme peel to rid the skin of any dead cell buildup and follow up with a hydrating mask that will replenish the water content of your skin."
"Please skip the moisturizer. I have oily skin and I don't like the shine."	"It may sound counterintuitive, but excessive oil in skin doesn't replace loss of moisture. In fact, proper moisturizing can actually reduce the oily appearance because it contributes to a better balance of oil and moisture in the skin. May I recommend a moisturizer that's formulated for oily skin?"
"I can't seem to get rid of these pimples and blackheads. I've tried so many different products!"	"That sounds frustrating. Any combination of conditions may be responsible, such as improper cleansing, hormonal imbalance, stress and even humid weather. "Let's begin with a treatment program aimed at addressing your concerns. Your facial will include a deep cleanse and specific exfoliation to help with removal of blackheads and surface debris that may be clogging your pores. If the condition continues, your physician or a dermatologist may be able to determine if other factors may be contributing to your acne."
"I need to return this moisturizer. It makes the skin in my cheek area break out."	"I'm so sorry to hear that. I've never had that happen before. Is it possible that it could be your blush? This moisturizer is water-based and non-comedogenic, which doesn't generally cause a breakout. Yet it's very common for the dyes and colors in makeup to do just that, especially if, as in your case, it's only along the cheek area. Why don't you continue with the moisturizer for just one more week and discontinue your current blush. If you're still having a problem, I'll certainly exchange it."

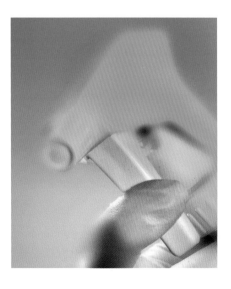

SKIN CARE INFECTION CONTROL AND SAFETY

It is your responsibility as a professional to protect your client by following infection control and safety guidelines with any and all services you provide.

Cleaning is a process of removing dirt, debris and potential pathogens to aid in slowing the growth of pathogens. Cleaning is performed prior to disinfection procedures.

Disinfection methods kill certain pathogens (bacteria, viruses and fungi) with the exception of spores. Disinfectants are available in varied forms, including concentrate, liquid, spray or wipes that are approved EPA-registered disinfectants available for use in the salon industry. Complete immersion and the use of disinfecting spray or wipes are the most often used practices when it comes to disinfecting tools, multi-use supplies and equipment in the salon. Be sure to follow the manufacturer's directions for mixing disinfecting solutions and contact time, if applicable.

SKIN CARE CLEANING AND DISINFECTION

Keep in mind that only nonporous tools, supplies and equipment can be disinfected. All single-use items must be discarded after each use. Always follow your area's regulatory guidelines.

TOOLS/SUPPLIES	FUNCTION	CLEANING GUIDELINES	DISINFECTION GUIDELINES
SPATULA	» Removes product from containers	» If single-use item – Must be discarded. » If multi-use item – Preclean with soap and water; rinse well.	» If multi-use item – Disinfect by immersing in an approved EPA-registered disinfectant solution. » Rinse well.
GLOVES	» Protect hands	» Single-use item; must be discarded.	» Cannot be disinfected.
FAN BRUSH	» Applies product on face or neck	» Preclean with soap and water. » Rinse well.	» Immerse in an approved EPA-registered disinfectant solution. » Rinse well.
HEADBAND OR HEAD COVERING	» Keeps hair off of client's face » Keeps product out of client's hair	» Remove hair and debris. » Wash in washing machine after each use.	» Use an approved laundry additive if required by area's regulatory agency. » Dry thoroughly.
MIXING BOWLS	» Hold mixtures for any type of peel or mask prior to applying to the skin	» Preclean with soap and water. » Rinse well.	» Immerse in an approved EPA-registered disinfectant solution. » Rinse well.

TOOLS/SUPPLIES	FUNCTION	CLEANING GUIDELINES	DISINFECTION GUIDELINES
SHEETS, BLANKETS	» Provide warmth and comfort to client	» Remove hair and debris. » Wash in washing machine after each use.	» Use an approved laundry additive if required by regulatory agency. » Dry thoroughly.
CLIENT ROBE/GOWN	» Allows client to remove clothing to keep it clean	» Remove hair and debris. » Wash in washing machine after each use.	» Use an approved laundry additive if required by area's regulatory agency. » Dry thoroughly.
TOWEL	» Cushions client's head » Keeps hair protected » If wet and warm, removes mask product	» Remove hair and debris. » Wash in washing machine after each use.	» Use an approved laundry additive if required by area's regulatory agency. » Dry thoroughly.
COTTON PADS/SWABS	» Remove product from face and neck	» Single-use item; must be discarded.	» Cannot be disinfected.
FACIAL TISSUE	» Removes lipstick » Blots face after toning	» Single-use item; must be discarded.	» Cannot be disinfected.

Store disinfected tools and multi-use supplies in a clean, dry, covered container or cabinet.

EQUIPMENT	FUNCTION	PRECAUTIONS
FACIAL STEAMER	» Uses warm, humid mist to open pores for cleansing » Softens dead skin cells for easier removal » Causes increased blood circulation by making the blood vessels expand » Improves cell metabolism	» Use only distilled or filtered water to clean out container each day. » Water level should be in compliance with the manufacturer's directions. » Average distance from client's face is 16-18" (40-50 cm). » Adjust ventilating systems to avoid interfering with the flow of the steam.
MAGNIFYING LAMP	» Provides thorough examination of skin's surface, using magnification and glare-free light » Beneficial when analyzing the skin	» Be aware of the electrical cord with floor-standing model.
INFRARED LAMP	» Provides a soothing heat that penetrates into the tissues of the body » Relaxes the client » Softens the skin to allow penetration of product and increases blood flow	» Be aware of the electrical cord with floor-standing model. » Average distance from client is 30" (75 cm).
WOOD'S LAMP	» Allows analysis of skin surface and deeper layers to aid in determining treatment by using deep ultraviolet light of the lamp » Different colors will indicate various conditions	» Do not allow the lamp to overheat. » Avoid direct contact between the lamp and skin. » Do not look directly at the bulb while it is being used.
VACUUM	» Creates mild suction » Increases circulation to the surface » Helpful in deep-pore cleansing	» Do not use on clients who are pregnant or who have high blood pressure or heart problems.

Equipment is disinfected by wiping it down with an approved EPA-registered disinfectant spray or wipe.

EQUIPMENT (CONT'D)	FUNCTION	PRECAUTIONS
HIGH-FREQUENCY CURRENT MACHINE 	» Creates current that is thermal, or heat producing, and germicidal	» Do not clean glass electrodes with alcohol just before using, as it is flammable. » Do not use on clients who are pregnant or who have high blood pressure or heart problems.
FACIAL BED 	» Holds client	» Ensure the adjustable bed is locked in position before inviting client to lie down.

Equipment is disinfected by wiping it down with an approved EPA-registered disinfectant spray or wipe.

Alert! If tools, multi-use supplies or equipment have come in contact with blood or body fluids, the following disinfection procedures must take place: **»** **Use an approved EPA-registered hospital disinfectant according to manufacturer's directions and as required by your area's regulatory agency.**

SALON**CONNECTION**

T.E.A.M.: Together Everyone Achieves More

It's essential to keep the spa area clean in order to provide a safe and comfortable environment for your clients. But when it comes to keeping it clean, some people simply do not remember what to do, and as a result, don't do anything at all! Using the proper infection control procedures for all tools, supplies and equipment at the right time can prevent major health risks for your clients.

If you notice a co-worker not following your area's regulated infection control guidelines, it's a good idea to offer help with how to properly clean/disinfect the items. Remember—if regulators come to audit your salon and one person did it wrong, the entire salon will suffer the consequences.

CARE AND SAFETY

Below is a list of safety precautions you should always adhere to prior and during basic facial services. These precautions will protect you and the client and ensure a safe work environment.

Personal Care	Client Care Prior to the Service	Client Care During the Service	Salon Care
>> Check that your personal standards of hygiene minimize the spread of infection.	>> Drape client using the cocoon wrap.	>> Use eye pads to protect and soothe the eyes when analyzing the skin or applying masks.	>> Follow health and safety guidelines, including cleaning and disinfecting procedures.
>> Wash hands and dry thoroughly with a single-use towel.	>> Use clean linens with each new client.	>> Be aware of skin sensitivity.	>> Ensure equipment, including the chair, sink, table and counter areas are clean and disinfected before and after every service.
>> Disinfect workstation.	>> Identify contraindications (conditions or factors that serve as reasons to withhold certain treatments). Possible conditions include: ▓ High blood pressure ▓ Heart problems ▓ Diabetes ▓ Pregnancy ▓ Pacemaker or metal implants ▓ Medications	>> Work carefully around nonremovable jewelry/piercings.	>> Promote a professional image by assuring your workstation is clean and tidy throughout the service.
>> Clean and disinfect tools appropriately.	>> Keep lids tightly closed on product jars to avoid spillage and contamination.	>> Be aware of nonverbal cues the client may be conveying.	>> Keep tools dry to avoid a short circuit when using electrical equipment.
>> Wear single-use gloves, as required.	>> Complete skin care record form and skin evaluation form.	>> Remove all products from jars with a clean spatula.	>> Keep labels on all containers and store products in a cool place to protect shelf life.
>> Refer to your area's regulatory agency for proper mixing/handling of disinfectant solution.		>> If any tools or multi-use supplies are dropped, be sure to pick them up, then clean and disinfect.	>> Clean/mop water spillage from floor to avoid accidental falls.
>> Minimize fatigue by maintaining good posture during the services.		>> Store soiled towels in dry, covered receptacle until laundered.	

Draping — Cocoon Wrap

For the client's safety and protection, follow proper draping guidelines for all facial services.

Drape cotton blanket over facial bed and position white cotton sheet over blanket. Lay one flat towel and one folded towel at the top of the bed for client's head. Have client lay on top of the sheet.

1. Fold one edge of blanket/sheet combination toward middle of bed
2. Repeat with the other edge, overlapping at center
3. Wrap the end of the blanket/sheet under the client's feet
4. Tuck towel over top of cocoon wrap

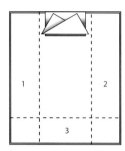 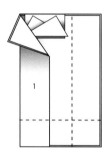 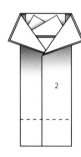 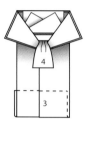

SKIN CARE PRODUCTS

Safety Data Sheets (SDS) for all products used in the salon should be easily available for your use.

PRODUCTS	FUNCTION
Cleanser	Removes impurities from the skin's surface
Toner	Helps further cleanse, soothe and smooth the skin while bringing it to a normal pH
Chemical Exfoliant	Removes dead skin cells by using enzymes and hydroxy acids
Mechanical Exfoliant	Removes dead skin cells by methods, such as facial cloths, scrubs or a brush
Massage Cream/Oil	Reduces friction and provides "slip" to the skin during massage
Masks	Cleanse, hydrate, tighten pores, exfoliate, reduce excess oil or offer nourishment to the skin
Moisturizer	Hydrates and protects the skin
Sunscreen	Protects the skin from UV rays or sun exposure

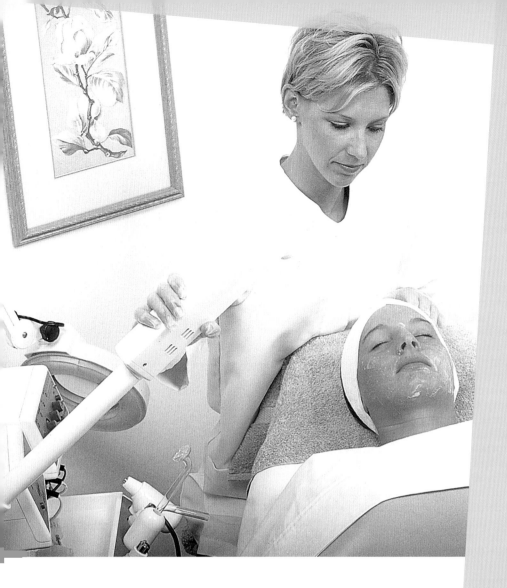

BASIC FACIAL SERVICE OVERVIEW

The Basic Facial Service Overview identifies the three areas of all skin care services:

>> The Basic Facial Preparation provides a brief overview of the steps to follow *before* you actually begin the basic facial service.

>> The Basic Facial Procedure provides an overview of the procedures that you will use *during* the basic facial service to ensure predictable results.

>> The Basic Facial Completion provides an overview of the steps to follow *after* performing the basic facial service to ensure guest satisfaction.

BASIC FACIAL SERVICE OVERVIEW

BASIC FACIAL PREPARATION	>> Clean and disinfect workstation and facial bed. >> Arrange appropriate facial tools and supplies. >> Wash hands. >> Ask client to remove jewelry; store in a secure place.

BASIC FACIAL PROCEDURE	>> Drape client for the service using the cocoon wrap.
	>> **Remove makeup** from client's face:
	  ▪ Use cotton pads to remove eye shadow
	  ▪ Use cotton swab to remove eyeliner
	  ▪ Use facial tissue or a gauze pad to remove lip color, if applicable
	>> **Apply cleanser** to client's face using smooth, sweeping strokes:
	  ▪ Obtain cleanser with a clean spatula (or pump) to prevent cross-contamination; apply to both hands
	  ▪ Begin at neck/chin and work up toward the forehead
	  ▪ Remove cleanser beginning at neck, working upward
	  ▪ Repeat cleanser application and removal, if required
	>> **Apply toner** using a piece of cotton to restore pH and aid in cleansing of the skin.
	>> Place eye pads over client's eyes.
	>> **Analyze client's skin** using magnifying lamp to check for skin abrasions, excessive oil, flakiness and clogged pores. This will help determine skin type and aid in recommending additional services and retail products.
	>> **Apply appropriate exfoliant** according to manufacturer's directions:
	  ▪ Work from neck to forehead
	  ▪ Avoid eyelids and mouth
	  ▪ Enzyme exfoliant may require facial steamer (generally 10 minutes)
	  ▪ Remove exfoliant by wrapping a warm steam towel wrap from chin to forehead (without covering the mouth and nose) and gently remove exfoliant from forehead to chin. (Option: Use damp disposable sponges or moist cotton pads)
	>> **Apply massage cream** to client's face and neck; perform massage movements without breaking contact with client's skin:
	  ▪ *Forehead:* Hand-over-hand effleurage (ring fingers); half-circle movements (middle fingers)
	  ▪ *Eyes:* Pause with slight pressure at temples; tapotement around eyes; circle outside of eyes (ring fingers); small circular movements at temples
	  ▪ *Nose:* Massage outer corners of nose; slide fingers up side of nose; apply pressure to eye sockets; repeat three times; scissor movements with index and middle fingers; repeat three times
	  ▪ *Cheeks:* Tapotement in a circular motion
	  ▪ *Mouth:* Slightly lift corners of mouth upward three times; massage in circular motion around mouth three times; perform scissor movements with index finger above mouth and middle finger below mouth
	  ▪ *Chin:* Repeat scissor movement
	  ▪ *Jawline:* Circular movements using thumb and index finger
	  ▪ Work back up toward the forehead using circular movements and effleurage on sides of face
	  ▪ Remove massage cream with cotton pads and warm water beginning at the neck
	>> **Apply facial mask** with a fan brush beginning at the neck:
	  ▪ Allow mask to set (generally 10 minutes)
	  ▪ Remove mask with warm steam towel wrap and cotton pads
	>> **Apply toner.**
	>> **Apply sun protection and moisturizing cream** using effleurage movements.

BASIC FACIAL COMPLETION	>> Reinforce client's satisfaction with overall salon experience. >> Make professional product recommendations. >> Prebook client's next appointment. >> End client's visit with warm and personal goodbye. >> Discard single-use supplies; disinfect tools and multi-use supplies; disinfect workstation and arrange in proper order. >> Complete client record. >> Wash hands.

BASIC FACIAL RUBRIC

A performance rubric is a document that identifies defined criteria at which levels of performance can be measured objectively. The Basic Facial Rubric is an example that your instructor might choose to use for scoring. The Basic Facial Rubric is divided into three main areas–Preparation, Procedure and Completion. Each area is further divided into step-by-step procedures that will ensure client safety and satisfaction.

BASIC FACIAL RUBRIC   Allotted Time: 45 Minutes

Student Name:_____ ID Number: _____

Instructor: _____ Date: _____ Start Time: _____ End Time: _____

BASIC FACIAL (Live Model) – *Each scoring item is marked with either a "Yes" or a "No." Each "Yes" counts for one point. Total number of points attainable is 28.*

CRITERIA	YES	NO	INSTRUCTOR ASSESSMENT
PREPARATION: *Did student…*			
1. Set up workstation with properly labeled supplies?	☐	☐	
2. Place disinfected tools and supplies at a visibly clean workstation?	☐	☐	
3. Wash their hands?	☐	☐	
Connect: *Did student…*			
4. Meet and greet client with a welcoming smile and pleasant tone of voice?	☐	☐	
5. Communicate to build rapport and develop a relationship with client?	☐	☐	
6. Refer to client by name throughout service?	☐	☐	
Consult: *Did student…*			
7. Ask questions to discover client's wants and needs?	☐	☐	
8. Analyze client's skin and review record for any possible contraindications to service?	☐	☐	
9. Gain feedback and consent from client before proceeding?	☐	☐	
PROCEDURE: *Did student…*			
10. Properly drape client (cocoon wrap) and prepare for service?	☐	☐	
11. Use products economically?	☐	☐	
Create: *Did student…*			
12. Cleanse face, obtain cleanser with clean spatula, apply cleanser with both hands and remove cleanser with cotton pads and warm water?	☐	☐	
13. Apply toner to skin surface with piece of cotton?	☐	☐	
14. Place eye pads over client's eyes and analyze client's skin using the magnifying lamp?	☐	☐	
15. Apply appropriate exfoliant product; remove exfoliant with warm steam towel or cotton pad?	☐	☐	
16. Obtain massage cream; apply massage cream; perform massage movements; remove massage cream with cotton pads and warm water?	☐	☐	
17. Apply facial mask with a fan brush; allow mask to set; remove mask with warm steam towel and cotton pads?	☐	☐	
18. Apply toner to skin surface with piece of cotton?	☐	☐	
19. Apply sun protection and moisturizing cream to skin surface using effleurage movements?	☐	☐	
COMPLETION *(Complete):* *Did student…*			
20. Ask questions and look for verbal and nonverbal cues to determine client's level of satisfaction?	☐	☐	
21. Make professional product recommendations?	☐	☐	
22. Ask client to make a future appointment?	☐	☐	
23. End client's visit with a warm and personal goodbye?	☐	☐	
24. Discard single-use supplies?	☐	☐	
25. Disinfect tools and multi-use supplies; disinfect workstation and arrange in proper order?	☐	☐	
26. Complete service within scheduled time?	☐	☐	
27. Complete client record?	☐	☐	
28. Wash their hands following service?	☐	☐	

COMMENTS: _____   TOTAL POINTS = _____ ÷ 28 = _____ %

Remember, your client's comfort and safety depend on you. Professionals are licensed and trusted to perform high-quality services that keep clients coming back to experience it again and again.

LESSONS LEARNED

>> The service essentials related to skin care are:

- Connect: Establish rapport and builds credibility with each client

- Consult: Analyze client needs, complete skin evaluation and obtain client consent

- Create: Ensure client safety and comfort; stay focused to deliver the best service; explain the products to your client; teach the client at-home care maintenance

- Complete: Request feedback; recommend products; suggest future appointment times; complete client record

>> Examples of infection control and safety guidelines for skin care services could include:

- Wash hands and wear gloves during treatments, as required.

- Use freshly cleaned linens with each new client.

- Identify contraindications, which are conditions or factors that serve as reasons to withhold certain treatments.

- Use eye pads to protect and soothe the eyes when analyzing the skin or applying masks.

- Remove all products from jars with a clean spatula.

- Store disinfected tools and multi-use supplies in a clean, dry, covered container or cabinet.

- Clean and disinfect the chair, sink, table and counter area before and after every service with an approved EPA-registered disinfectant.

- Keep labels on all containers, and store products in a cool place to protect shelf life.

>> Products used for skin care services include:

- Cleanser – Removes impurities

- Toner – Returns skin to a normal pH

- Exfoliant (Chemical/Mechanical) – Removes dead skin

- Massage Cream/Oil – Reduces friction during massage

- Masks – Cleanse, hydrate, tighten pores, exfoliate, reduce excess oil or offer nourishment

- Moisturizer – Hydrates and protects

- Sunscreen – UV protection

>> The three areas of a basic facial service are:

- Preparation – Provides a brief overview of the steps to follow before you actually begin the basic facial service.

- Procedure – Provides an overview of the procedures that you will use during the basic facial service to ensure predictable results.

- Completion – Provides an overview of the steps to follow after performing the basic facial service to ensure guest satisfaction.

BASIC FACIAL

EXPLORE

Why do you think clients book a salon facial, instead of just cleansing their skin at home?

INSPIRE

Increasing your knowledge of skin care services will help you advise clients and recommend spa services.

ACHIEVE

Following this *Basic Facial Workshop*, you'll be able to:

>> Explain and demonstrate steps used during a basic facial, including massage techniques

PERFORMANCE GUIDE

BASIC FACIAL

View the video, then perform this workshop. Complete the self-check as you progress through the workshop.

45 mins
Suggested Salon Speed

PREPARATION ✔

>> Assemble tools, supplies and products
>> Set up workstation
>> Wash your hands
>> Wear gloves if required by your area's regulating agency

☐

CLEANSE AND TONE

1. **Drape client and apply headband.** ☐

2. **Remove eye makeup using eye makeup remover:** ☐
   >> Use cotton pad to remove eye shadow
   >> Perform downward and inward strokes
   >> Use cotton swab to remove eyeliner

3. **Remove lipstick using a gauze pad or tissue:** ☐
   >> Work from outer corner to center on both sides of lips

4. **Obtain cleanser:** ☐
   >> Use a clean spatula
   >> Apply cream to both hands

5. **Apply cleanser evenly over face and neck using both hands:** ☐
   >> Use smooth, sweeping strokes
   >> Be consistent, do not remove hands from face until cleansing is complete
   >> Follow the **Product Application Movements** in step 6

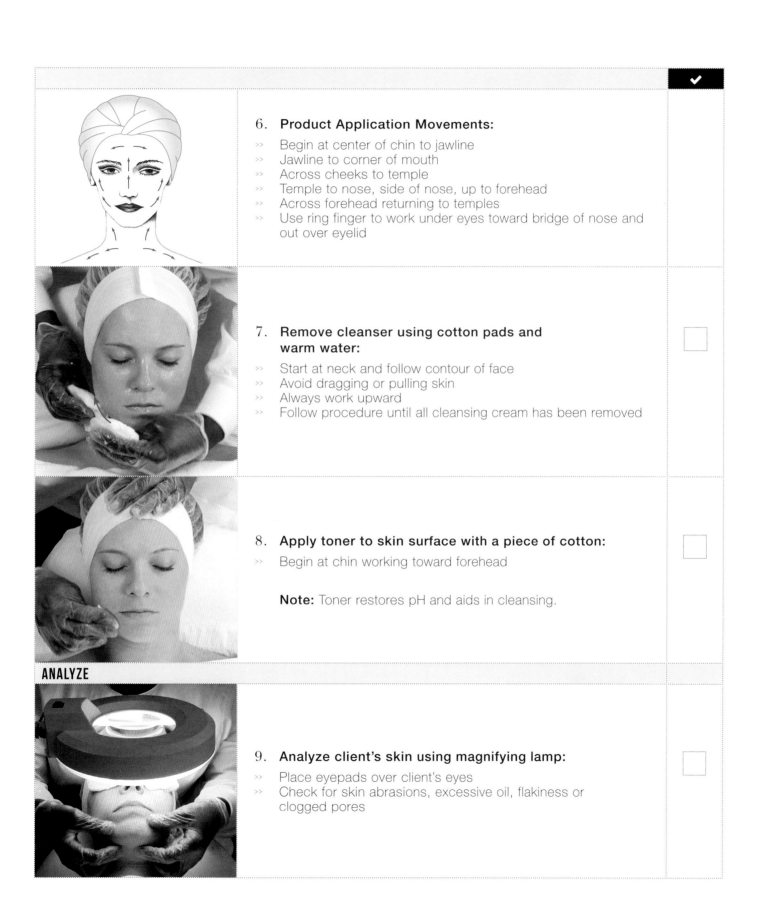

6. **Product Application Movements:**

>> Begin at center of chin to jawline
>> Jawline to corner of mouth
>> Across cheeks to temple
>> Temple to nose, side of nose, up to forehead
>> Across forehead returning to temples
>> Use ring finger to work under eyes toward bridge of nose and out over eyelid

7. **Remove cleanser using cotton pads and warm water:**

>> Start at neck and follow contour of face
>> Avoid dragging or pulling skin
>> Always work upward
>> Follow procedure until all cleansing cream has been removed

8. **Apply toner to skin surface with a piece of cotton:**

>> Begin at chin working toward forehead

Note: Toner restores pH and aids in cleansing.

ANALYZE

9. **Analyze client's skin using magnifying lamp:**

>> Place eyepads over client's eyes
>> Check for skin abrasions, excessive oil, flakiness or clogged pores

EXFOLIATE ✔

10. Apply exfoliant to client's skin:

>> Work from neck toward forehead
>> Avoid eyelids and mouth
>> Always follow manufacturer's directions
>> Granular scrub
  ▪ Massage in small circular movements
>> Alpha hydroxyl acid
  ▪ Allow product to remain on skin for given amount of time
>> Enzyme exfoliant
  ▪ Steam for approximately 10 minutes

11. Remove exfoliant using warm steam towel wrap or cotton pads:

>> Release steam from towel
>> Test temperature of towel before applying
>> Apply towel beginning at chin and wrap around face up the eyes and forehead
>> Do not cover mouth and nose
>> Gently pat down towel to absorb some of product
>> Wipe away exfoliant working from forehead to chin using towel

Note: When removing a chemical exfoliant, use tepid water and cotton pads.

MASSAGE

12. Apply massage cream:

>> Obtain with clean spatula
>> Apply to both hands
>> Apply to entire face following the **Product Application Movements** in step 6
>> Work from chin to forehead
>> Apply enough lotion to avoid running out during massage movements

13. Perform massage movements:

>> Massage face using effleurage, petrissage, tapotement, friction and vibration movements
>> Refer to **Massage Movements Chart** on next page

MASSAGE MOVEMENTS CHART

Massage techniques and movements are varied. The movements listed below are considered a foundation that you can build on to create your own unique pattern.

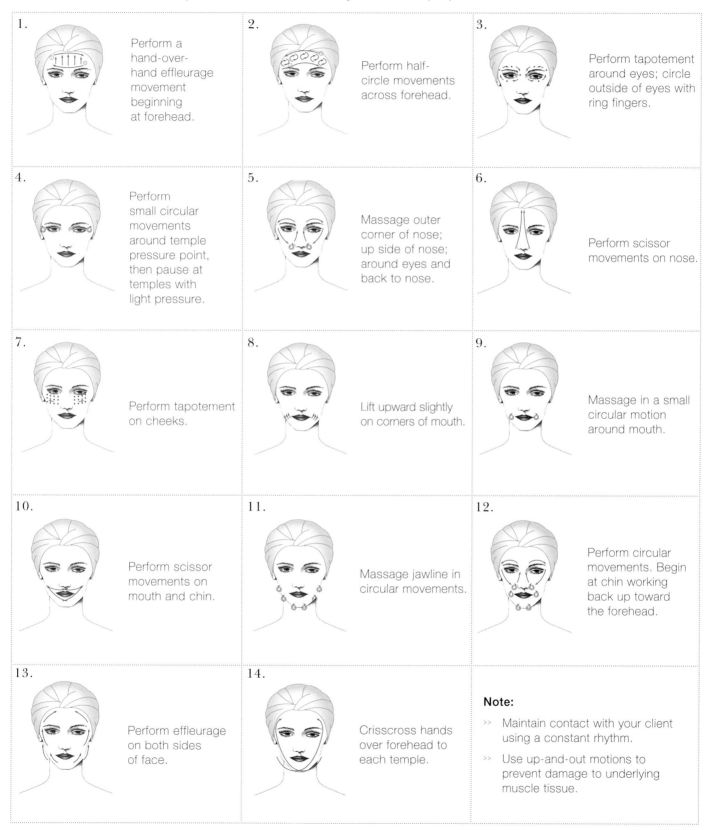

1. Perform a hand-over-hand effleurage movement beginning at forehead.

2. Perform half-circle movements across forehead.

3. Perform tapotement around eyes; circle outside of eyes with ring fingers.

4. Perform small circular movements around temple pressure point, then pause at temples with light pressure.

5. Massage outer corner of nose; up side of nose; around eyes and back to nose.

6. Perform scissor movements on nose.

7. Perform tapotement on cheeks.

8. Lift upward slightly on corners of mouth.

9. Massage in a small circular motion around mouth.

10. Perform scissor movements on mouth and chin.

11. Massage jawline in circular movements.

12. Perform circular movements. Begin at chin working back up toward the forehead.

13. Perform effleurage on both sides of face.

14. Crisscross hands over forehead to each temple.

Note:

>> Maintain contact with your client using a constant rhythm.

>> Use up-and-out motions to prevent damage to underlying muscle tissue.

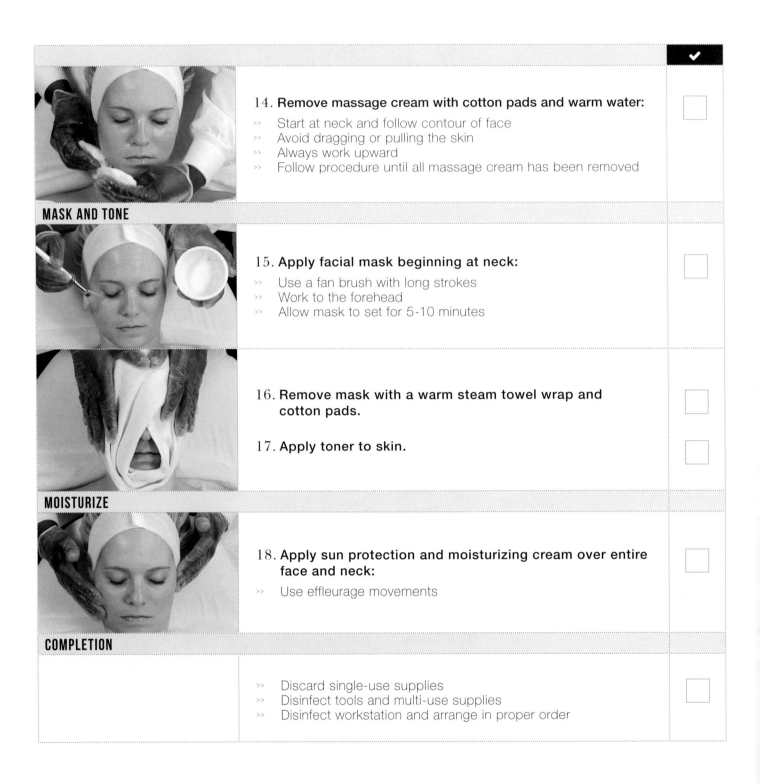

✓

14. **Remove massage cream with cotton pads and warm water:**
>> Start at neck and follow contour of face
>> Avoid dragging or pulling the skin
>> Always work upward
>> Follow procedure until all massage cream has been removed

MASK AND TONE

15. **Apply facial mask beginning at neck:**
>> Use a fan brush with long strokes
>> Work to the forehead
>> Allow mask to set for 5-10 minutes

16. **Remove mask with a warm steam towel wrap and cotton pads.**

17. **Apply toner to skin.**

MOISTURIZE

18. **Apply sun protection and moisturizing cream over entire face and neck:**
>> Use effleurage movements

COMPLETION

>> Discard single-use supplies
>> Disinfect tools and multi-use supplies
>> Disinfect workstation and arrange in proper order

45 mins
Suggested Salon Speed

My Speed
_____
_____
_____

INSTRUCTIONS:
Record your time in comparison with the suggested salon speed. Then, list here how you could improve your performance.

_____

_____

_____

_____

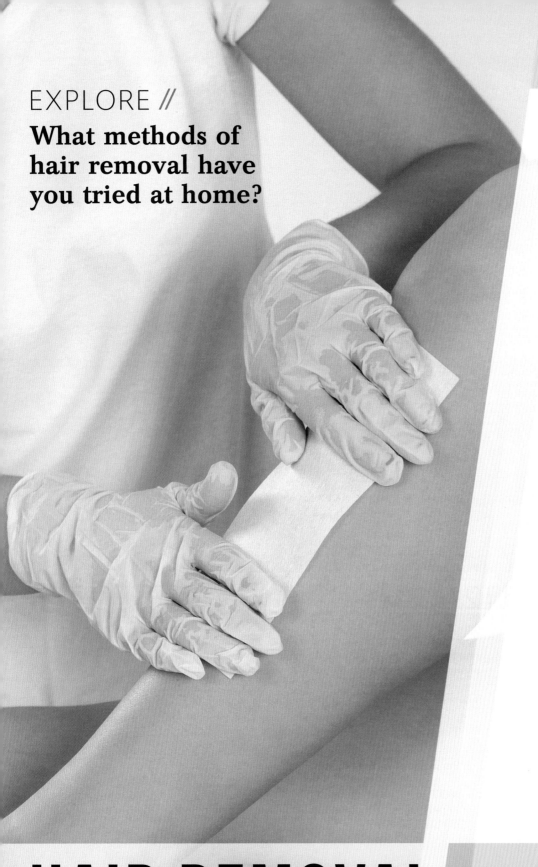

What methods of hair removal have you tried at home?

As a professional, you'll have the ability to offer clients longer-lasting hair removal results.

ACHIEVE //

Following this lesson on *Hair Removal Theory*, you'll be able to:

>> Describe the six different methods of temporary hair removal

>> Compare laser hair reduction and photoepilation

FOCUS //

HAIR REMOVAL THEORY

Temporary Hair Removal

Permanent Hair Reduction

HAIR REMOVAL
112.6 THEORY

>> **Hypertrichosis (hi-per-tri-KOH**-sis) **– The condition of unwanted or superfluous hair**

>> **Hirsutism (HER**-se-tizm) **–** Condition where women grow dark hair in areas of the body that men typically grow more hair

112.6 | HAIR REMOVAL THEORY

Society and personal preferences have long dictated a person's need or desire for removing unwanted or superfluous hair. As a salon professional, you will recommend the best way to remove the unwanted hair or make it less visible.

There are two categories of hair removal:

>> **Temporary hair removal**

>> **Permanent hair reduction** (requires electricity)

NOTE: Additional, specialized training is required for salon professionals to perform permanent hair reduction services. An overview is included in this lesson.

TEMPORARY HAIR REMOVAL

Temporary hair removal is a common practice. Often, clients may choose to perform some techniques themselves at home:

>> Shaving

>> Chemical depilatories

>> Tweezing

Or they may choose to see a salon professional for:

>> Waxing

>> Threading

>> Sugaring

With some techniques, hair can grow back in a matter of hours or days, such as with shaving; in other instances hair grows back in several weeks, as with waxing.

SHAVING

The hair removal method most often used when unwanted hair covers large areas, such as women's legs, is **shaving**. Keep in mind that this service is usually performed by the client at home.

Shaving can be performed using:
>> Electric shaver
>> Clippers
>> Razor

When using a razor:
>> Apply water and shaving cream before the service to make the skin and hair softer and to reduce the potential for skin irritations.

>> Use moisturizing lotion or cream after the service to keep the skin soft and help eliminate dryness or flaking.

As the hair grows back it may feel more coarse or thicker due to the blunt effect of the razor. Shaving unwanted hair at the nape hairline can be done with the clippers or razor. Be guided by your regulatory agency's laws regarding shaving the skin.

CHEMICAL DEPILATORIES

A **chemical depilatory** is a painless method of hair removal that dissolves the hair at skin level. The main ingredient of these products is a thioglycolic acid derivative, with an alkaline pH, that chemically softens and degrades the protein structure of the hair. Once the disulfide bonds are broken, the softened mass of hair can be scraped away.

Chemical depilatories are usually found in one of the following forms:
>> Cream
>> Paste
>> Powder (which is designed to be mixed)

NOTE: An allergy test needs to be given to determine sensitivity to any depilatory product prior to use. A reaction, such as itching, burning or inflammation, is a negative indication of product use. Always read and follow the manufacturer's instructions.

Chemical depilatories are most often used as home treatments and not commonly used in salons. However, if performing a chemical depilatory service in the salon, prepare for this hair removal service by assembling the materials, preparing the workspace and following the infection control guidelines throughout the service.

EPILATION

Epilation is the removal of hair from the follicle. Unlike shaving and a chemical depilatory, which remove the hair above skin level, epilation happens under the skin when the hair is removed from the follicle. A few examples of epilation methods include:

>> Tweezing
>> Waxing
>> Threading
>> Sugaring
>> Electrolysis
>> Laser
>> Photoepilation

TWEEZING

Tweezing is the hair removal method most commonly used to remove unwanted hairs from smaller areas, such as:

» Eyebrows

» Chin

» Around the mouth

It would be too time-consuming and painful to use this method on larger areas of the body. Any client that prefers tweezing as their primary hair removal method may need standing appointments as frequently as once a month since the results typically last 4-6 weeks. Note that tweezing can be very beneficial in finishing the eyebrow design.

To tweeze, an individual hair is grasped with the tweezers and removed in the direction of hair growth, extracting it from beneath the skin's surface from the base of the follicle.

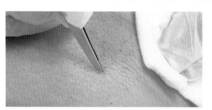

SHAPING THE EYEBROWS

The curved line (orbital bone) of the eye socket serves as a guide for the natural arch of the eyebrow. While the shape of your client's eyebrows needs to be customized for facial features, follow these general guidelines to achieve a well-arched eyebrow whether you are tweezing or waxing.

» The brow should begin over the inside corner of the eye.

» The peak, or highest point of the arch, should occur over the outside of the iris of the eye.

» Imagine a diagonal line from the outside of the nose that extends past the outside of the eye. This point is where the brow should end.

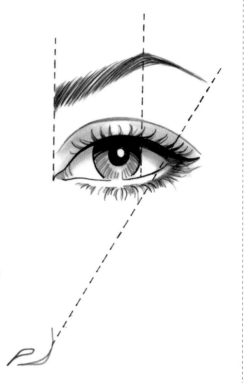

Eyebrow Tweezing Service Guidelines

A good brow design creates a frame for the face and "opens" the eye. A person with excessive hair may benefit from waxing instead of tweezing because it is faster and less irritating.

» **Assemble materials** and prepare workspace.

» **Wash hands.**

» **Cleanse** area to be tweezed.

» **Analyze your client's brows** using the shaping guidelines above; consider the client's overall appearance before you determine how thick or thin the eyebrows should be.

» **Brush the hairs up** with a brow brush; this will allow you to see the base of the hairs and to remove them in neat rows rather than at random.

» **Hold the skin taut** with one hand by stretching it between the thumb and index finger; **tweeze the hairs in the direction of hair growth**, using quick movements.

» **Tweeze stray hairs** that appear above and below the natural brow line.

» To create a more pronounced arch, tweeze in an upward direction from just inside the beginning of the brow to the area you determined should be the highest point of the arch.

» Continue tweezing, sloping gently downward, toward the outer edge of the brow; the points you choose to begin and end your arch and the degree of slope you create will determine how pronounced the arch will be.

» **Complete one brow**, then the other, making sure they match.

» **Apply toner** to the area, then apply a soothing cream.

» **Offer to prebook a visit** within a 4-6 week period.

» Return to service area and **perform necessary infection control procedures.**

WAXING

One of the most requested hair removal services professionals perform is waxing. **Waxing is a service in which the hair is physically removed from the follicle by applying the wax, allowing the hair to firmly adhere to the wax, then pulling off the wax, which removes the imbedded hair.** Waxing is a procedure that is beneficial for temporarily removing hair from both large and small areas. **There are two types of wax:**

>> **Soft (Strip)**

>> **Hard (Non-strip)**

CONTRAINDICATIONS FOR WAXING

Prior to waxing, you should review any possible contraindications that might suggest you avoid performing the service. Typically, these will be included on the Client Consultation Form. Skin diseases that present visible irritation on the surface of the skin should never be waxed. Waxing over these areas may cause skin irritation or can spread viruses or bacteria to other areas. Some contraindications include:

SKIN CONDITIONS, DISEASES AND DISORDERS	HEALTH CONDITIONS	ORAL OR TOPICAL MEDICATIONS/TREATMENTS
>> Varicose veins	>> Diabetes	>> Accutane
>> Unusually pronounced moles and warts	>> Poor circulation	>> Antibiotics
>> Cuts, abrasions, wounds, open sores	>> Chemotherapy/radiation treatments	>> Cortisone creams
>> Active herpes	>> Low pain threshold	>> Retin-A/Renova
>> Acne	>> Lupus	>> Alpha hydroxy acids and beta hydroxy acids (AHAs and BHAs)
>> Sunburn	>> Client is taking a blood thinner	>> Chemical peels
>> Rashes		>> Laser treatments
>> Cysts or boils		>> Microdermabrasion
>> Rosacea		>> Recent cosmetic surgery

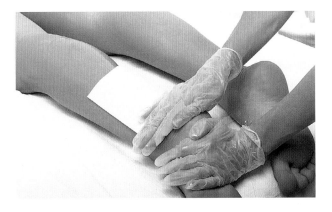

Soft (Strip) Wax

The majority of professional waxing services are performed with soft wax (also known as a classic wax and strip wax) because hair removal over large areas can be accomplished quickly and easily with this type of wax. Soft wax is melted in a heated wax pot, applied to the skin in a thin layer with a spatula and covered with strips. The material is then lifted off the skin, opposite the direction of hair growth, removing the wax and hair simultaneously.

Basic Soft Wax Guidelines

It is important to understand that the general procedure documented here is the same for waxing any area of the body:

- >> Wash hands.

- >> Wear protective single-use gloves if required by your area's regulatory agency.

- >> Assess direction of hair growth.

- >> Apply cleansing gel or antiseptic preparation.

- >> Lightly dust the area with powder (talc) if recommended by manufacturer.

- >> Obtain wax.

- >> Apply wax at 45° angle in direction of hair growth.

- >> Discard the spatula.

- >> Apply removal strip; press and smooth strip.

- >> Hold skin taut and remove strip parallel to skin, against natural growth.

- >> Apply pressure.

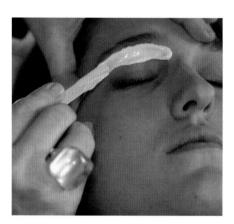

Photo courtesy of Cirépil

Hard Wax

This wax usually is ideal for small areas and thinner, more sensitive skin. It is also an option for clients who can't tolerate soft wax. The application of hard wax is similar to a soft wax application—apply in the direction of growth. When removing hard wax, strips are not used; instead, the wax itself is pulled opposite the direction of the hair growth. Used hard wax should be disposed of after every client.

WHEN WAXING:

- >> Always check the temperature of the wax on the inside of your wrist

- >> Never double-dip the spatula

- >> Advise client not to suntan immediately following a waxing service

- >> Avoid waxing vellus (lanugo) hair since it may cause the skin to lose its softness

Basic Hard Wax Guidelines

It is important to understand that the general procedure documented here is the same for waxing any area of the body:

- >> Wash hands.

- >> Wear protective single-use gloves if required by your regulating agency.

- >> Assess direction of hair growth.

- >> Apply cleansing gel or antiseptic preparation.

- >> Obtain wax.

- >> Apply wax at 45° angle in direction of hair growth.

- >> Discard spatula.

- >> Hold skin taut; remove wax against hair growth.

- >> Apply pressure.

THREADING

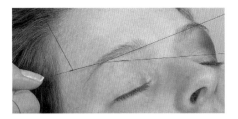

Threading, also known as banding, is an ancient method of hair removal that utilizes 100% cotton thread that is twisted and rolled along the surface of the skin. The results last approximately 4-6 weeks—the same as with tweezing—and the side effects can be less severe than with other hair removal methods. Threading has gained popularity recently and requires additional specialized training.

SUGARING

Sugaring is a hair removal technique that utilizes a paste made primarily of sugar that is applied to the skin in a rolling motion. When removed with a strip, it takes the hair along with it. Sugar paste adheres only to the hair, not the skin, and is easily removed with water. Sugaring provides the same results as soft or hard wax. A benefit of sugaring is that hair as short as ⅛" (.3 cm) long can be removed.

Selecting the appropriate hair removal method for each body area is easy using the following chart.

METHOD	BODY AREA
» Waxing	» Face
	» Upper lip
	» Eyebrows
	» Underarms/arms
	» Bikini line
	» Back/shoulders
	» Legs
	» Tops of feet/toes
» Tweezing	» Face
	» Upper lip
	» Eyebrows
» Depilatories	» Arms
	» Back/shoulders
	» Legs
	» Tops of feet/toes

SALON**CONNECTION**

Male Grooming

Men also get waxing services…they're just not as likely to brag about it! Common waxing services for men are eyebrows, back and chest.

PERMANENT HAIR REDUCTION

Methods of permanent hair reduction that are used by professionals trained in these particular areas are:

1. Electrolysis

2. Light

NOTE: Most regulating agencies will not license a salon professional to perform permanent hair reduction without additional specialized training. Be guided by your regulating agency's requirements.

ELECTROLYSIS

Permanent hair reduction, known as electrolysis, uses electric current to damage the cells of the papilla and disrupt hair growth. The goal is to damage enough papilla (growth) cells so that either a lighter, finer-diameter hair grows back or, ideally, no hair grows from the follicle at all. Several treatments per follicle (exposure to current) are normally required before lasting results are achieved. In most areas, this method is performed by a licensed professional called an electrologist. An electrologist has advanced training specifically in the study of electrolysis or is a medical doctor.

The medical community recognizes three methods of electrolysis:

1. Galvanic electrolysis or multiple-needle process

2. Thermolysis or high frequency/short-wave method

3. Blend, a combination of galvanic and thermolysis

Each of these methods has advantages and disadvantages. Remember, advanced training is required to perform electrolysis in most areas.

The American Electrology Association states that electrolysis is the only method approved by the FDA for permanent reduction of unwanted hair. As the hair is treated, regrowth is prevented rather than just removed temporarily. Only electrolysis provides both hair removal and hair elimination.

Galvanic Method

The galvanic electrolysis method destroys the hair by decomposing the papilla.

>> Multiple wire needles or probes are inserted into the follicle.

>> A low level of current passes into the needles and causes a chemical reaction in the cells of the papilla.

>> The current is typically on from 30 seconds to 2½ minutes.

>> The instrument has multiple probes that are normally inserted with minimal discomfort and activated at one time; for this reason, galvanic electrolysis is sometimes called the **multiple-needle process.**

Thermolysis Method

The thermolysis or high frequency/short-wave method involves inserting a single needle (probe) into the follicle.

>> The current travels to the papilla for less than a second, resulting in a coagulation of the cells.

>> The hair is immediately tweezed from the follicle.

>> The time and intensity of the current are carefully controlled, preferably by an automatic timer; the client feels only a tiny "flash" of heat.

>> Redness or a slight bump in the skin are normal reactions and disappear in two or three days.

>> The wire used in thermolysis is substantially finer than the electrolysis probe, further reducing client discomfort.

Blend Method

The **blend method** of hair removal is a combination of galvanic and thermolysis technology.

>> A special instrument designed to combine galvanic current (for best results on resistant follicles) and high frequency current (for faster results) produce the blend.

>> Highly trained electrologists may use this method if the other methods fail.

>> The advantages and disadvantages are similar to those of the individually used methods.

>> This method is a "last chance" alternative for clients with excessive or resistant hair growth.

DISCOVER**MORE**

Hair Removal Alternative

If your client wants hair to be less visible without having it removed, consider lightening the hair. You can use a prepared product designed to lighten hair on the face or arms, or you can mix one part oil lightener with two parts hydrogen peroxide. Apply mixture to the area to be lightened and monitor until hair has lightened to the desired shade (15-60 minutes, depending on the hair's color and texture). Thoroughly rinse off lightener and cleanse area. Apply a moisturizing cream.

LIGHT

There are many methods that use a light-based system to permanently reduce hair growth. It is important to have knowledge of the different methods that clients refer to as "laser hair removal." Two methods are covered in this lesson:

>> Laser hair reduction

>> Photoepilation

Light-based treatments are only effective when hair is in the anagen phase of growth.

LASER IS AN ACRONYM:

Light
Amplification
Simulated
Emission
Radiation

Laser Hair Reduction

Laser hair reduction treatments use wavelengths of light to penetrate and diminish or destroy hair bulbs. Laser hair reduction systems emit a beam of light that passes through the skin to the hair follicle. The hair absorbs the light and transforms it into heat energy, which destroys the hair bulb. The benefit of the laser is that it can treat hundreds of hair follicles simultaneously, generally making the process quicker than electrolysis. However, certain clients are not good candidates for this type of hair reduction procedure; because lasers pinpoint melanin, the hair being treated must be darker than the surrounding skin color for the best result. Generally, laser is recommended for clients with coarse, dark hair, which responds best to laser treatments. Some clients will see permanent hair reduction while other clients will see slower hair regrowth.

Depending on the local area regulations, laser hair reduction can be performed by licensed estheticians, medical professionals, or by technicians under a doctor's supervision.

Photoepilation

Photoepilation or intense pulsed light (IPL) uses a similar principle as lasers, but this type of light is not considered to be a laser light. An intense, pulsed light beam creates a burst of energy used to destroy hair bulbs with minimal scarring. Both lasers and pulsed light are a form of light beam. The difference between the two is that a laser is a constant beam of light and the pulsed is not constant, it contains multiple wavelengths. Both methods carry the risk of scarring, but there is much less chance of burning or scarring when using pulsed light since it is targeted at the skin in quick, short intervals. The benefit of this type of treatment is that large areas of the body such as the back or legs can be treated rapidly. Photoepilation can provide 50% to 60% clearing of hair over a 12-week period of time.

LESSONS LEARNED

>> The six methods of temporary hair removal can be described as:

- Shaving – Used at home; used when unwanted hair covers large areas

- Chemical depilatory – Painless method of hair removal that dissolves the hair at skin level

- Tweezing – Method most commonly used to remove unwanted hairs from smaller areas

- Waxing – Hair is physically removed from the follicle by applying the wax, allowing the hair to firmly adhere to the wax and pulling off the wax, which removes the imbedded hair

- Threading – Utilizes 100% cotton thread that is twisted and rolled along the surface of the skin to remove hair

- Sugaring – Utilizes a paste made primarily of sugar that is applied to the skin in a rolling motion to remove hair

>> Laser hair removal and photoepilation are both a form of permanent hair reduction that is achieved with a light. The light of a laser is a constant beam where photoepilation (intense pulsed light) is not constant and contains many wavelengths.

EXPLORE //

Have you ever heard the saying, "It hurts to be beautiful"?

HAIR REMOVAL
GUEST EXPERIENCE
112.7

112.7 | HAIR REMOVAL GUEST EXPERIENCE

INSPIRE //

While some hair removal services can sting, you can maximize your clients' comfort during the experience.

ACHIEVE //

Following this lesson on *Hair Removal Guest Experience,* you'll be able to:

>> Identify the service essentials related to hair removal services

>> Summarize the tools and essentials related to hair removal

>> Provide examples of infection control and safety guidelines for hair removal services

>> Explain the three areas of a hair removal service

FOCUS

HAIR REMOVAL GUEST EXPERIENCE

Hair Removal Service Essentials

Hair Removal Infection Control and Safety

Hair Removal Service Overview

Hair Removal Rubrics

W hether your client is getting ready for the sleeveless season, desiring a more natural browline or requesting detailed attention to an upper lip, you have an opportunity to offer an exceptional guest experience. Clients will return for future hair removal services if you pay attention to the details related to the services you are providing. Remember to remind them how much more comfortable and convenient their life will be as a result of the service they experienced today.

HAIR REMOVAL SERVICE ESSENTIALS

As with all professional services, consulting with your client prior to the actual service will ensure predictable results and will help you avoid any misunderstandings. As you review the four basic steps of the hair removal service essentials, remember the importance of active listening, critical thinking and analysis of the overall success of the service.

CONNECT

>> Meet and greet the client with a welcoming smile and a pleasant tone of voice.

>> Communicate to build rapport and develop a relationship with the client.

>> Have client fill out a hair removal record form.

CONSULT

>> Ask questions to discover client's wants and needs.

>> Analyze client's skin where hair will be removed.

>> Assess the facts and thoroughly think through your recommendations after reading completed hair removal record form.

>> Explain your recommended solutions, the products that will be used and the price of the service.

>> Think not only of today's service, but future services also.

>> Gain feedback and consent from your client.

CREATE

>> Ensure client comfort during service.

>> Stay focused on delivering the service to the best of your ability.

COMPLETE

>> Request satisfaction feedback from your client.

>> Ask your client for referrals for future services.

>> Offer appreciation to your client and offer to prebook their next visit to the school or salon.

>> Record recommended products on client record form for future visits.

HAIR REMOVAL INFECTION CONTROL AND SAFETY

It is your responsibility as a professional to protect your client by following infection control and safety guidelines with any and all services you provide.

Cleaning is a process of removing dirt, debris and potential pathogens to aid in slowing the growth of pathogens. Cleaning is performed prior to disinfection procedures.

Disinfection methods kill certain pathogens (bacteria, viruses and fungi) with the exception of spores. Disinfectants are available in varied forms, including concentrate, liquid, spray or wipes that are approved EPA-registered disinfectants available for use in the salon industry. Immersion, and the use of disinfecting spray or wipes are the most often used practices when it comes to disinfecting tools, multi-use supplies and equipment in the salon. Be sure to follow the manufacturer's directions for mixing disinfecting solutions and contact time if applicable.

CLEANING AND DISINFECTION GUIDELINES

Keep in mind that only nonporous tools, supplies and equipment can be disinfected. All single-use items must be discarded after each use. Always follow your area's regulatory guidelines.

TOOLS, SUPPLIES AND EQUIPMENT	FUNCTION	CLEANING GUIDELINES	DISINFECTION GUIDELINES
Small Scissors	» Trim hair before and/or after the service	» Remove hair and debris. » Open hinged area to allow for thorough cleaning. » Pre-clean with soap and water.	» Use an approved EPA-registered disinfectant solution, wipe or spray.
Brow Brush	» Combs brow hair prior to shaping	» Remove hair and debris. » Pre-clean with soap and water.	» Immerse in an approved EPA-registered disinfectant solution.
Tweezers	» Remove stray hairs	» Remove hair and debris. » Pre-clean with soap and water.	» Immerse in an approved EPA-registered disinfectant solution.
Wax Warmer (Pot)	» Melts and holds wax	» Remove any wax drippings from the pot.	
Removal Strips	» Aid in removing hair; applied over wax	» Single-use item; must be discarded.	» Cannot be disinfected.
Spatula	» Removes wax from container/warmer; spreads the wax	» If single-use item – Discard.	» If multi-use item – Immerse in an approved EPA-registered disinfectant solution.

TOOLS, SUPPLIES AND EQUIPMENT	FUNCTION	CLEANING GUIDELINES	DISINFECTION GUIDELINES
Gloves	» Protect the hands	» Single-use item; must be discarded.	» Cannot be disinfected.
Sheet	» Protects the facial bed	» Remove hair and debris. » Wash in washing machine after each use.	» Use an approved laundry additive if required by area's regulatory agency. » Dry thoroughly.
Headband	» Holds hair out of the way	» Remove hair and debris. » Wash in washing machine after each use.	» Use an approved laundry additive if required by area's regulatory agency. » Dry thoroughly.
Plastic Bag	» Holds garbage	» Single-use item; must be discarded.	» Cannot be disinfected.
Soft Single-Use Towel	» Aids in removal of products	» Single-use item; must be discarded.	» Cannot be disinfected.
Facial Bed or Chair	» Holds client	» Remove sheet.	» Wipe down bed/chair with a disinfectant wipe.
Handheld Mirror	» Allows client to view results		» Use an approved EPA-registered disinfectant wipe.

Store disinfected tools and multi-use supplies in a clean, dry, covered container or cabinet.

CARE AND SAFETY

Infection control and safety guidelines are essential while performing hair removal services in order to protect the health and well-being of you and your client. Good-to-remember points in this area are: 1) Be guided by your area's regulatory agency; and 2) Read and follow manufacturer's directions.

Personal Care	Client Care Prior to the Service	Client Care During the Service	Salon Care
» Check that your personal standards of hygiene minimize the spread of infection.	» Seat client in comfortable position for the service.	» Be aware of skin sensitivity.	» Follow health and safety guidelines, including cleaning and disinfecting procedures.
» Wash hands and dry thoroughly with a single-use towel.	» Analyze the skin and area in need of hair removal.	» Do not use wax over moles; warts; irritated, abraded or sunburned skin; bruises or varicose veins.	» Ensure equipment, including facial chair, is clean and disinfected.
» Disinfect workstation.	» Cleanse the area.	» Work carefully around nonremovable jewelry/piercings.	» Promote a professional image by assuring your workstation is clean and tidy throughout the service.
» Clean and disinfect tools appropriately.	» Be sure to inquire what products are used at home prior to waxing.	» Keep products away from the client's eyes.	» Disinfect all tools after each use. Always use disinfected tools, supplies and equipment for each client.
» Wear single-use gloves as required.	» Handle tools and product with care.	» Do not rewax sensitive areas.	» Dispose of used wax after each client.
» Refer to your area's regulatory agency for proper mixing/handling of disinfectant solution.	» If any tools are dropped be sure to pick them up, then clean and disinfect.	» Do not re-dip spatula.	
» Minimize fatigue by maintaining good posture during the services.	» Test temperature of wax on inside of your wrist.	» Be aware of nonverbal cues the client may be conveying.	
» Carefully read and follow manufacturers' instructions for tools, supplies, products and equipment.	» Perform an allergy test prior to service.	» Store soiled towels in a dry, covered receptacle until laundered.	

To perform a professional hair removal service, you need a selection of products. Safety Data Sheets (SDS) for all products used in the salon need to be available.

PRODUCTS	FUNCTION
Cleansing Gel	Removes dirt and oil
Antiseptic	Product that can be applied to the skin to reduce microbes
Wax	Removes unwanted hair
Wax Remover	Cleans wax residue
Soothing Toner, Gel or Lotion (Post-Epilation Product)	Calms the skin after waxing
Powder (Talc)	Prevents wax from adhering to skin
Chemical Depilatory	Removes unwanted hair (cream formula generally)

HAIR REMOVAL SERVICE OVERVIEW

The Hair Removal Service Overview identifies the Preparation, Procedure and Completion areas for all hair removal services.

>> The Hair Removal Preparation provides a brief overview of the steps to follow *before* you actually begin the hair removal service.

>> The Hair Removal Procedure provides an overview of the removal procedures that you will use *during* the service to ensure predictable results.

>> The Hair Removal Completion provides an overview of the steps to follow *after* performing the hair removal service to ensure guest satisfaction.

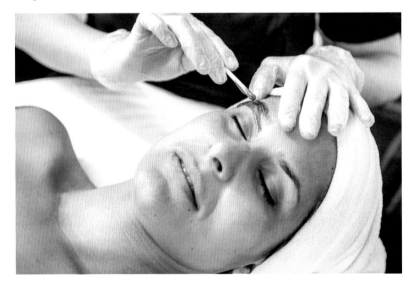

EYEBROW SOFT WAX SERVICE OVERVIEW

EYEBROW SOFT WAX PREPARATION	>> Clean and disinfect workstation. >> Cut removal strips. >> Arrange disinfected waxing tools, supplies and products. >> Warm up wax at least 30 minutes before client arrives. >> Wash hands and put on gloves. >> Perform analysis of area to be waxed. >> Ask client to remove jewelry; store in a secure place.

EYEBROW SOFT WAX PROCEDURE	>> Drape client for the service.
	>> Cleanse area to be waxed.
	>> Apply powder on area to be waxed to prevent wax from adhering to skin.
	>> Test temperature of wax on inside of your wrist.
	>> **Apply wax** at a 45° angle in direction of hair growth and discard spatula:
	  ▪ Even, thin layer under the eyebrow, where hair removal is desired.
	  ▪ Do not double-dip spatula; discard and use a new spatula each time more wax needs to be obtained.
	>> Apply **removal strip.**
	>> **Gently press and smooth** strip in direction of hair growth:
	  ▪ **Hold skin taut and remove** strip quickly in the opposite direction.
	  ▪ Pull strip along the skin, do not pull upward (Note: Pulling upward may cause bruising).
	>> Apply **pressure** immediately to minimize pain and redness.
	>> Apply **antiseptic** if slight bleeding or irritation occurs:
	  ▪ Antiseptic helps prevent bacterial growth.
	>> **Remove wax** residue with wax remover.
	>> **Remove wax remover** with a soft single-use towel.
	>> **Apply soothing toner, gel or lotion** to calm the skin.
	>> **Tweeze** to remove stray hairs.

EYEBROW SOFT WAX COMPLETION	>> Reinforce client's satisfaction with overall salon experience. >> Make professional product recommendations. >> Prebook client's next appointment. >> End client's visit with warm and personal goodbye. >> Discard single-use supplies; disinfect tools and multi-use supplies; disinfect workstation and arrange in proper order. >> Complete client record. >> Wash hands.

HAIR REMOVAL RUBRICS

A performance rubric is a document that identifies defined criteria at which levels of performance can be measured objectively. The following rubrics are examples that your instructor might choose to use for scoring. Each hair removal rubric is divided into three main areas—Preparation, Procedure and Completion. Each area is further divided into step-by-step procedures that will ensure client safety and satisfaction.

EYEBROW SOFT WAX RUBRIC

Allotted Time: 30 Minutes

Student Name:_____ ID Number: _____

Instructor: _____ Date: _____ Start Time: _____ End Time: _____

EYEBROW SOFT WAX (Live Model) – *Each scoring item is marked with either a "Yes" or a "No." Each "Yes" counts for one point. Total number of points attainable is 33.*

CRITERIA	YES	NO	INSTRUCTOR ASSESSMENT
PREPARATION: *Did student…*			
1. Set up workstation and facial chair/bed with properly labeled supplies and products?	☐	☐	
2. Place disinfected tools and supplies at a visibly clean workstation?	☐	☐	
3. Wash their hands?	☐	☐	
Connect: Did student…			
4. Meet and greet client with a welcoming smile and pleasant tone of voice?	☐	☐	
5. Communicate to build rapport and develop a relationship with client?	☐	☐	
6. Refer to client by name throughout service?	☐	☐	
Consult: Did student…			
7. Ask questions to discover client's wants and needs?	☐	☐	
8. Analyze area to be waxed?	☐	☐	
9. Check for any contraindications?	☐	☐	
10. Gain feedback and consent from client before proceeding?	☐	☐	
PROCEDURE: *Did student…*			
11. Properly drape client and prepare for service?	☐	☐	
12. Use products economically?	☐	☐	
Create: Did student…			
13. Cleanse the area to be waxed with a cleansing gel?	☐	☐	
14. Apply powder (talc) to the eyebrow area?	☐	☐	
15. Test the temperature of the wax on inside of wrist prior to application?	☐	☐	
16. Apply a thin, even layer of wax at a 45° angle along the area to be waxed?	☐	☐	
17. Apply wax in the direction of hair growth?	☐	☐	
18. Apply removal strip and gently press and smooth it in the direction of hair growth?	☐	☐	
19. Hold skin taut and quickly remove strip in the opposite direction?	☐	☐	
20. Apply pressure to waxed area immediately after removal?	☐	☐	
21. Remove wax residue with a wax remover?	☐	☐	
22. Remove wax remover with a soft single-use towel?	☐	☐	
23. Apply soothing lotion, toner or gel to waxed area?	☐	☐	
24. Tweeze stray hairs if necessary?	☐	☐	
COMPLETION (*Complete*): *Did student…*			
25. Ask questions and look for verbal and nonverbal cues to determine client's level of satisfaction?	☐	☐	
26. Make professional product recommendations?	☐	☐	
27. Ask client to make a future appointment?	☐	☐	
28. End client's visit with a warm and personal goodbye?	☐	☐	
29. Discard single-use supplies?	☐	☐	
30. Disinfect tools and multi-use supplies; disinfect workstation and facial chair/bed and arrange in proper order?	☐	☐	
31. Complete service within scheduled time?	☐	☐	
32. Complete client record?	☐	☐	
33. Wash their hands following service?	☐	☐	

COMMENTS: _____ TOTAL POINTS = _____ ÷ 33 = _____ %

LEG SOFT WAX SERVICE OVERVIEW

**LEG
SOFT WAX
PREPARATION**

>> Clean and disinfect workstation.
>> Cut and/or arrange removal strips.
>> Arrange disinfected waxing tools, supplies, products and equipment.
>> Warm up wax at least 30 minutes before client arrives.
>> Wash hands and put on gloves.
>> Perform analysis of area(s) to be waxed.
>> Ask client to remove jewelry; store in a secure place.

**LEG
SOFT WAX
PROCEDURE**

>> Drape client for the service.
>> Cleanse area to be waxed; use hands to apply to large areas like the legs.
>> Apply powder on area to be waxed to prevent wax from adhering to skin.
>> Test temperature of wax on inside of your wrist.
>> **Apply wax** at a 45° angle in direction of hair growth on front of legs; discard spatula:
   ▪ Distribute an even, thin layer in rows with a sweeping motion.
   ▪ Do not double-dip spatula; discard and use a new spatula each time more wax needs to be obtained.
>> Apply **removal strip.**
>> **Gently press and smooth** strip in direction of hair growth:
   ▪ **Hold skin taut and remove** strip quickly in the opposite direction.
   ▪ Pull strip along the skin, do not pull upward (Note: Pulling upward may cause bruising).
>> Apply **pressure** immediately to minimize pain and redness.
>> Repeat, be sure to work quickly so wax does not cool and harden.
>> Remove all wax in each section before repeating on a new row or section as you complete the front of both legs.
>> Repeat waxing procedures on back of both legs.
>> Apply **antiseptic** if slight bleeding or irritation occurs:
   ▪ Antiseptic helps prevent bacterial growth.
>> **Remove wax** residue with wax remover.
>> **Remove wax remover** with a soft single-use towel.
>> **Apply soothing toner, gel or lotion** to calm the skin.
>> **Tweeze** to remove stray hairs.

**LEG
SOFT WAX
COMPLETION**

>> Reinforce client's satisfaction with overall salon experience.
>> Make professional product recommendations.
>> Prebook client's next appointment.
>> End client's visit with warm and personal goodbye.
>> Discard single-use supplies; disinfect tools and multi-use supplies; disinfect workstation and arrange in proper order.
>> Complete client record.
>> Wash hands.

LEG SOFT WAX RUBRIC

Student Name:_____ ID Number: _____

Instructor: _____ Date: _____ Start Time: _____ End Time: _____

LEG SOFT WAX (Live Model) — *Each scoring item is marked with either a "Yes" or a "No." Each "Yes" counts for one point. Total number of points attainable is 35.*

CRITERIA	YES	NO	INSTRUCTOR ASSESSMENT
PREPARATION: *Did student...*			
1. Set up workstation and facial chair/bed with properly labeled supplies and products?	☐	☐	
2. Place disinfected tools and supplies at a visibly clean workstation?	☐	☐	
3. Wash their hands?	☐	☐	
Connect: *Did student...*			
4. Meet and greet client with a welcoming smile and pleasant tone of voice?	☐	☐	
5. Communicate to build rapport and develop a relationship with client?	☐	☐	
6. Refer to client by name throughout service?	☐	☐	
Consult: *Did student...*			
7. Ask questions to discover client's wants and needs?	☐	☐	
8. Analyze area to be waxed?	☐	☐	
9. Check for any contraindications?	☐	☐	
10. Gain feedback and consent from client before proceeding?	☐	☐	
PROCEDURE: *Did student...*			
11. Properly drape client and prepare for service?	☐	☐	
12. Use products economically?	☐	☐	
Create: *Did student...*			
13. Cleanse both legs with a cleansing gel using hands?	☐	☐	
14. Apply powder (talc) to the area(s) to be waxed?	☐	☐	
15. Test the temperature of the wax on inside of wrist prior to application?	☐	☐	
16. Apply a thin, even layer of wax at a 45° angle in separate rows with a sweeping motion?	☐	☐	
17. Apply wax in the direction of hair growth?	☐	☐	
18. Apply removal strip and gently press and smooth it in the direction of hair growth?	☐	☐	
19. Hold skin taut and quickly remove strip in the opposite direction?	☐	☐	
20. Apply pressure to waxed area immediately after removal?	☐	☐	
21. Work quick enough so that wax did not cool and harden?	☐	☐	
22. Repeat waxing techniques on the back of both legs?	☐	☐	
23. Remove wax residue with a wax remover?	☐	☐	
24. Remove wax remover with a soft single-use towel?	☐	☐	
25. Apply soothing lotion, toner or gel to waxed area?	☐	☐	
26. Tweeze stray hairs if necessary?	☐	☐	
COMPLETION (Complete): *Did student...*			
27. Ask questions and look for verbal and nonverbal cues to determine client's level of satisfaction?	☐	☐	
28. Make professional product recommendations?	☐	☐	
29. Ask client to make a future appointment?	☐	☐	
30. End client's visit with a warm and personal goodbye?	☐	☐	
31. Discard single-use supplies?	☐	☐	
32. Disinfect tools and multi-use supplies; disinfect workstation and facial chair/bed and arrange in proper order?	☐	☐	
33. Complete service within scheduled time?	☐	☐	
34. Complete client record?	☐	☐	
35. Wash their hands following service?	☐	☐	

COMMENTS: _____ TOTAL POINTS = _____ ÷ 35 = _____ %

SALON**CONNECTION**

MYTH OR FACT: The temperature of the heated wax kills bloodborne pathogens?

Myth – It does not. This is why you must NEVER double-dip: The temperature that the heated wax goes up to is not high enough to kill diseases.

DISCOVER**MORE**

Wax Color and Viscosity

Wax comes in different colors and viscosities! Some wax is for sensitive skin and some wax is for sensitive areas. Research different waxing manufacturers and record what their different colors and viscosities are, and which skin types they are for.

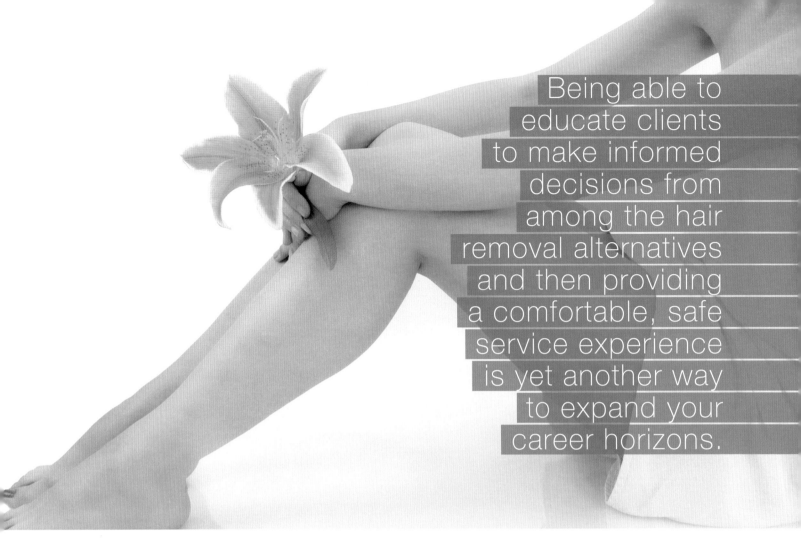

Being able to educate clients to make informed decisions from among the hair removal alternatives and then providing a comfortable, safe service experience is yet another way to expand your career horizons.

LESSONS LEARNED

>> The service essentials related to hair removal can be identified as:

- ▪ Connect – Meet and greet the client; communicate and build rapport

- ▪ Consult – Ask questions to determine client's needs

- ▪ Create – Ensure client comfort during service

- ▪ Complete – Suggest a future appointment time for your client's next visit; record recommended products on client record

>> To perform a hair removal service, tools, supplies and products need to be prepared and set up in a room with the proper equipment. Scissors, tweezers and the brow brush must be disinfected and stored in a dry, covered container. Finally, removal strips must be pre-cut and ready, prior to the service.

>> The following are some infection control and safety guidelines to follow during a hair removal service:

- ▪ Remove hair and debris from tools

- ▪ Disinfect tools with an EPA-registered disinfectant solution, wipe or spray

- ▪ Wash sheets and headbands

- ▪ Wipe down facial chair with a disinfectant wipe

- ▪ Wash hands and wear gloves during the service

- ▪ Perform an allergy test

- ▪ Test temperature of wax on inside of wrist

>> The three areas of a hair removal service are:

- ▪ Preparation – Provides a brief overview of steps to follow *before* you actually begin the service

- ▪ Procedure – Provides an overview of the removal procedures that you will use *during* the service

- ▪ Completion – Provides an overview of the steps to follow *after* performing the hair removal service

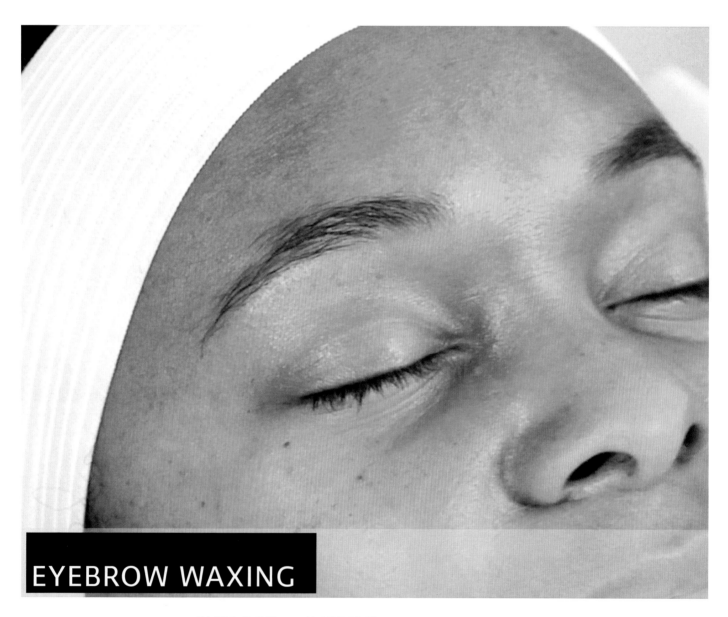

EYEBROW WAXING

EXPLORE

Have you ever felt compelled to groom someone's eyebrows?

INSPIRE

As a professional, it is your responsibility to recommend personal care services that will enhance your client's appearance.

ACHIEVE

Following this *Eyebrow Waxing Workshop*, you'll be able to:

>> Demonstrate proper procedures to perform an eyebrow wax service

EYEBROW WAXING

View the video, then perform this workshop. Complete the self-check as you progress through the workshop.

30 mins
Suggested
Salon Speed

PREPARATION	✔
>> Assemble tools, supplies and products >> Set up workstation >> Wash your hands >> Wear gloves if required by your area's regulating agency	☐

CLIENT/SKIN PREPARATION

1. **Drape client and apply headband.** ☐

2. **Examine area to be waxed:** ☐
   - >> Check for contraindications
   - >> Assess direction of hair growth
   - >> Determine desired brow shape
   - >> Identify hair to be removed

3. **Cleanse area with antiseptic gel:** ☐
   - >> Apply gel to cotton
   - >> Swipe cotton across eyebrows from inside to outside of eye

4. **Apply powder to eyebrow area.** ☐

   Note: Powder prevents wax from adhering to the skin when using soft (strip) wax.

EYES – BROWS – APPLY/REMOVE WAX ✓

5. **Apply thin layer of wax to unwanted hair:**
   >> Use clean spatula
   >> Position spatula at 45° angle
   >> Apply in direction of hair growth
   >> Discard spatula

   Note: Test temperature of wax on the inside of your wrist before you begin service to ensure client comfort.

6. **Apply removal strip:**
   >> Press down firmly in direction of hair growth

7. **Remove strip quickly in opposite direction of hair growth:**
   >> Hold skin taut
   >> Hold end of strip
   >> Pull across, not upward
   >> Apply pressure to skin immediately to minimize pain
   >> Apply an antiseptic if slight bleeding or irritation occurs

8. **Repeat waxing procedures, as needed, to complete and balance both brows.**

CLEAN AND PROTECT SKIN

9. **Remove excess wax remaining on eyebrow area with wax remover.**

10. **Apply soothing lotion with cotton to rehydrate skin.**

TWEEZE

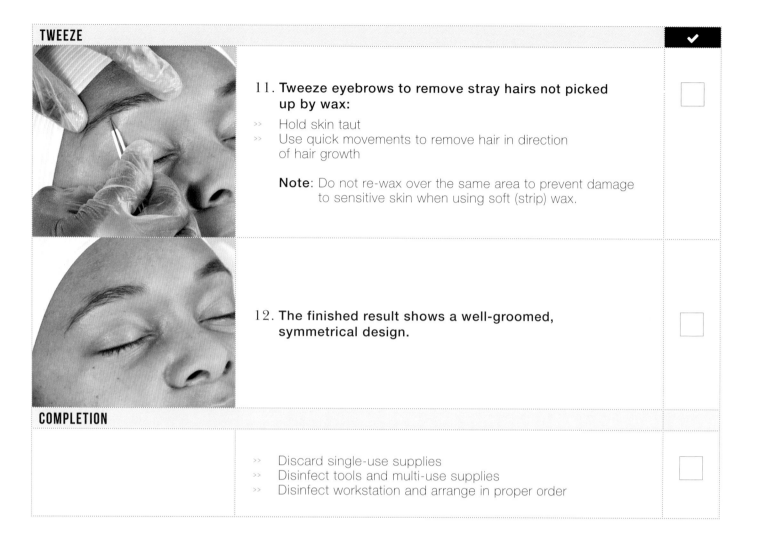

11. **Tweeze eyebrows to remove stray hairs not picked up by wax:**
>> Hold skin taut
>> Use quick movements to remove hair in direction of hair growth

   Note: Do not re-wax over the same area to prevent damage to sensitive skin when using soft (strip) wax.

12. **The finished result shows a well-groomed, symmetrical design.**

COMPLETION

>> Discard single-use supplies
>> Disinfect tools and multi-use supplies
>> Disinfect workstation and arrange in proper order

30 mins
Suggested Salon Speed

My Speed
_____
_____
_____

INSTRUCTIONS:

Record your time in comparison with the suggested salon speed. Then, list here how you could improve your performance.

_____
_____
_____
_____
_____

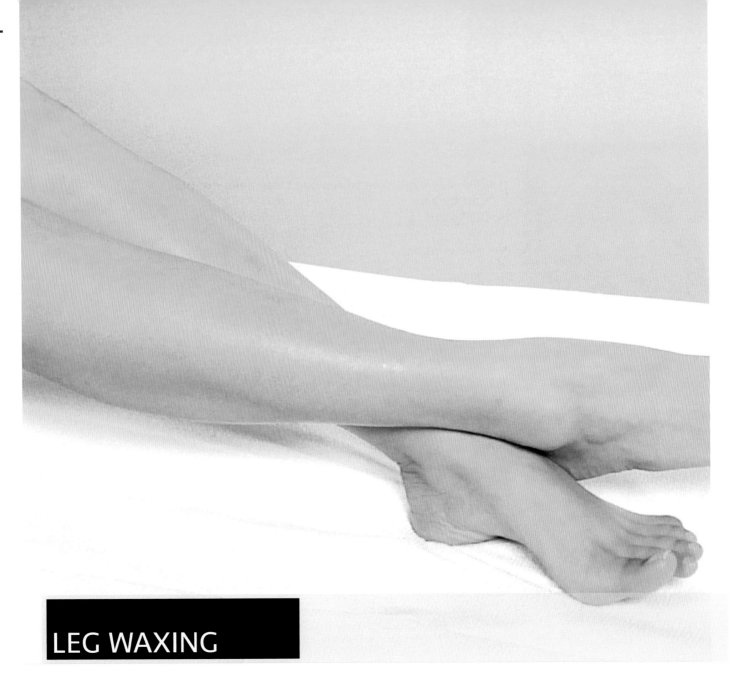

LEG WAXING

EXPLORE

Why would a client request a leg waxing procedure in the salon instead of shaving at home?

INSPIRE

The ability to perform cross-departmental services increases a new hairdresser's value to the salon.

ACHIEVE

Following this *Leg Waxing Workshop*, you'll be able to:

>> Demonstrate proper procedures to perform a leg wax service

LEG WAXING

View the video, then perform this workshop. Complete the self-check as you progress through the workshop.

45 mins
Suggested
Salon Speed

PREPARATION	✔
>> Assemble tools, supplies and products >> Set up workstation >> Wash your hands >> Wear gloves if required by your area's regulating agency	☐

CLIENT/SKIN PREPARATION

1. **Drape client to expose area to be waxed.** ☐

2. **Examine area to be waxed:** ☐
   >> Check for contraindications
   >> Assess direction of hair growth

3. **Cleanse area with antiseptic gel:** ☐
   >> Apply gel thoroughly to both legs using your hands

4. **Apply powder to both legs to remove oil and moisture.** ☐

   Note: Powder prevents wax from adhering to the skin when using a soft (strip) wax.

LEGS – FRONT – APPLY/REMOVE WAX ✔

5. Apply thin layer of wax to unwanted hair:
>> Use clean spatula
>> Position spatula at 45° angle
>> Apply in direction of hair growth
>> Distribute in rows with a sweeping motion
>> Discard spatula after every application

Note: Test temperature of wax on the inside of your wrist before you begin service to ensure client comfort.

6. Apply removal strip:
>> Press down firmly in direction of hair growth

7. Remove strip quickly in opposite direction of hair growth:
>> Hold skin taut
>> Hold end of strip
>> Pull across, not upward
>> Apply pressure to skin immediately to minimize pain
>> Work quickly enough so wax does not cool and harden
>> Apply an antiseptic if slight bleeding or irritation occurs

Note: Remove all wax in each section before repeating on a new row or section.

8. Repeat waxing procedure to complete the front of both legs.

LEGS – BACK – APPLY/REMOVE WAX

9. Repeat waxing procedures on back of both legs:
>> Have client turn over
>> Apply, then remove strip quickly in opposite direction of hair growth

Note: The strip may be applied diagonally in the center back of leg to follow direction of hair growth.

CLEAN AND PROTECT SKIN

10. **Remove excess wax remaining on legs with wax cleanser:**
    >> Apply cleanser to both legs
    >> Remove excess product with towel

11. **Apply soothing lotion to rehydrate skin:**
    >> Use disposable cotton pads
    >> Distribute evenly to both legs

TWEEZE

12. **Tweeze to remove stray hairs not picked up by wax:**
    >> Hold skin taut
    >> Use quick movements to remove hair in direction of hair growth

    Note: Do not re-wax over the same area to prevent damage to sensitive skin when using soft (strip) wax.

COMPLETION

>> Discard single-use supplies
>> Disinfect tools and multi-use supplies
>> Disinfect workstation and arrange in proper order

---

45 mins
Suggested Salon Speed

My Speed
_____
_____
_____

INSTRUCTIONS:

Record your time in comparison with the suggested salon speed. Then, list here how you could improve your performance.

_____
_____
_____
_____
_____

112.10
MAKEUP THEORY

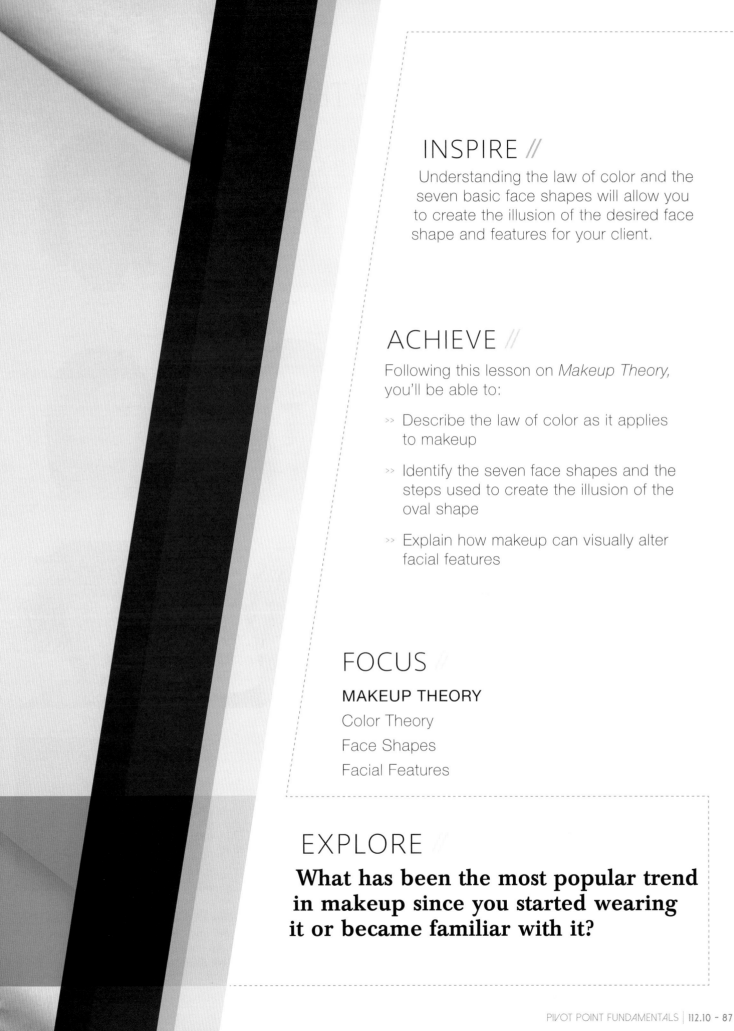

INSPIRE //

Understanding the law of color and the seven basic face shapes will allow you to create the illusion of the desired face shape and features for your client.

ACHIEVE //

Following this lesson on *Makeup Theory*, you'll be able to:

>> Describe the law of color as it applies to makeup

>> Identify the seven face shapes and the steps used to create the illusion of the oval shape

>> Explain how makeup can visually alter facial features

FOCUS //

MAKEUP THEORY

Color Theory

Face Shapes

Facial Features

EXPLORE //

What has been the most popular trend in makeup since you started wearing it or became familiar with it?

112.10 | MAKEUP THEORY

Trends in makeup change quickly, just like clothing and hair. The designs you create for your clients will vary from person to person and will relate to current trends, as well as the client's personal expression. Ideals of beauty vary from culture to culture and in different age groups. As your skill level increases, you may become more interested in other, more specific areas of makeup design. For example, designing makeup for photography, film and theater can be very challenging and rewarding.

Before

Before

Day

Day

Evening

Evening

Makeup design is about creating illusions. It utilizes an artistic concept called chiaroscuro. The basic premise of chiaroscuro is:

LIGHTER COLORS	DARKER COLORS
» Stand out	» Recede
» Accentuate	» Minimize
» Highlight attractive features	» Diminish less attractive features
» Emphasize areas that need to be "brought out"	» Shadow areas that you wish to minimize

Understanding the properties of darker and lighter colors allows you to visually alter the shape of the face. Also, by making the best use of "shine" and "matte" products you can enhance or diminish appropriately. Careful blending between lights and darks, as well as shine and matte, will help you to create the most effective illusions.

COLOR THEORY

Understanding the law of color is key when choosing and recommending the appropriate makeup color options for various skin, eye and hair color clients. The law of color states that out of all the colors in the universe, only three are pure. Colors are placed on a color wheel to show their relationships.

The three primary colors:
>> Red   >> Yellow   >> Blue

Mixing two primaries in varying proportions creates the three secondary colors:
>> Green   >> Orange   >> Violet

Mixing primary and secondary colors in varying proportions creates tertiary colors.
>> Yellow-green   >> Red-orange   >> Blue-green

>> Yellow-orange   >> Red-violet   >> Blue-violet

Colors opposite each other on the color wheel are called complementary colors.
>> Red is complementary of green.

>> Blue is complementary of orange.

>> Yellow is complementary of violet.

Complementary colors will neutralize each other when they are mixed together.

COLOR SCHEMES

Being familiar with color schemes will allow you to mix and blend colors to enhance client makeup designs.

Monochromatic color schemes use the same color (with variations in value and intensity) throughout the makeup design. (See blue-green shading on color wheel illustration.)

Analogous color schemes use three colors that are adjacent to each other on the color wheel; often used for day makeup designs. (See pink arrows on color wheel illustration.)

Triadic color schemes use three colors located in a triangular position on the color wheel and are often used for more vibrant makeup designs. (See blue arrows on color wheel illustration.)

Complementary color schemes use colors that are across from each other on the color wheel in order to achieve the greatest amount of contrast and are often used to enhance eye color.

Warm and **Cool** are terms used to describe the tones found in both skin colors and cosmetic colors. Warm colors have red or yellow tones within them, and cool colors have more blue tones within them.

Remember that dark colors seem to recede and diminish the appearance of certain features or areas, while lighter colors seem to advance, making features or areas appear larger or more prominent.

With the knowledge of color theory, face shapes and facial features, you'll be able to enhance your clients' best features while minimizing the less desirable ones.

DISCOVER**MORE**

The meaning of colors or symbolism behind colors is an interesting area to study. For example, what comes to your mind when you see the color red? People who have studied color share some of the following associations with different colors. See how your thoughts compare to their findings.

Red – Passion, love, danger, anger
Yellow – Happiness, optimism, creativity
Blue – Trust, dignity, intelligence, authority
Green – Growth, fertility, nature
Purple – Nobility, luxury
Orange – Energy, vitality, warmth

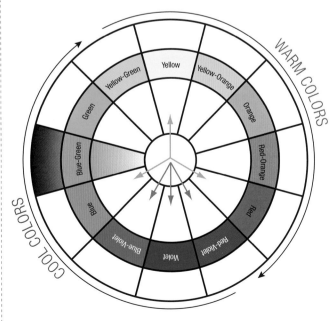

Color Wheel

TERMS YOU SHOULD KNOW

Hue is another term for color

Tint is a hue with white added

Shade is a hue with black added

Value is the lightness or darkness of a color

Intensity refers to the vibrancy of a color

Tone refers to the warmth or coolness of a color

FACE SHAPES

The well-proportioned oval face shape has long been considered the ideal or classic face shape. Standards of beauty have certainly expanded during recent decades, but most corrective makeup and contouring are done to achieve the illusion of an oval face. Face shapes other than the oval include round, square, oblong, pear, diamond and heart.

SEVEN BASIC FACE SHAPES

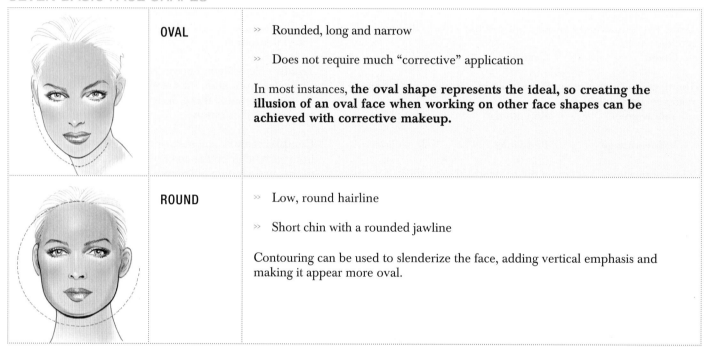

	OVAL	
	OVAL	» Rounded, long and narrow
		» Does not require much "corrective" application
		In most instances, **the oval shape represents the ideal, so creating the illusion of an oval face when working on other face shapes can be achieved with corrective makeup.**
	ROUND	» Low, round hairline
		» Short chin with a rounded jawline
		Contouring can be used to slenderize the face, adding vertical emphasis and making it appear more oval.

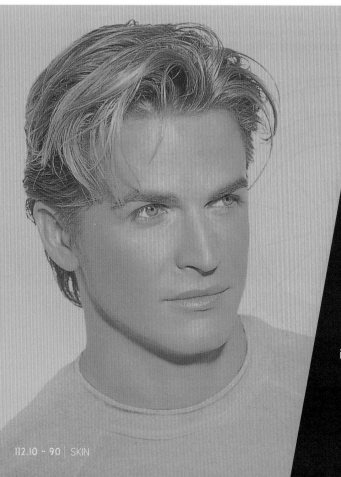

SALON**CONNECTION**

Male Esthetic Market

The male esthetic market is growing. More and more men are investing in skin care, grooming and cosmetic products to enhance skin health, camouflage flaws and promote a more youthful appearance. In fact, men represent one of the fastest growing consumer groups in both the spa and cosmetic surgery industries. Most men are interested in very simple skin care regimens to enhance the condition and appearance of their skin. As far as cosmetics are concerned, male clients may be open to products, such as skin bronzers, concealers and lip balms. When applying cosmetics to your male clients, always strive to enhance and balance features, promote even skin tone and camouflage imperfections. Do so with a light touch so that the cosmetics that you use appear as natural and subtle as possible.

	SQUARE	» Broad, straight forehead and hairline » Broad jawline » Angular, almost masculine Contouring can be done to soften the angularity and reduce the width.
	OBLONG (RECTANGLE)	» Long, narrow and angular » Wide jawline, almost horizontal This face can be visually shortened by contouring under the chin and horizontally at the hairline. Highlighting can be used to add visual width when possible. Horizontal lines should be emphasized whenever possible, in brow shape, cheek color and lip shape.
	PEAR (TRAPEZOID)	» Narrow forehead » Wide jawline Highlighting the forehead can add visual width, while contouring the bottom of the face can reduce width.
	DIAMOND	» Predominant width through cheekbones » Narrow forehead and chin/jaw areas The jaw and forehead can be made to look wider with highlighting, while width through the cheekbones can be minimized with contouring.
	HEART (TRIANGLE)	» Wider forehead » Narrow jaw or chin line The jawline can be visually widened with highlighting, while width across the forehead can be minimized by contouring.

FACIAL FEATURES

With the variety of face shapes and facial features, there will be times when a client wants to emphasize or minimize specific facial features. It is your job to communicate with the client to find out the areas that they would like to adjust visually. The placement of light and dark colors will allow you to create the illusion of the desired facial feature. Knowing how to apply makeup to suit different facial features is important in creating a more attractive makeup design. When following fashion trends, be sure that your makeup design is not accentuating less than perfect features.

	WIDE NOSE	**TO MAKE A WIDE NOSE LOOK NARROWER:** » Apply a darker tone/shade along side of nose. » Apply a lighter highlighter in a thin line down center of nose.
	LONG NOSE	**TO VISUALLY SHORTEN A LONG NOSE:** » Apply a darker shade to tip of nose.
	PROMINENT CHIN	**TO RECEDE A PROMINENT CHIN:** » Contour prominent area with a darker shade. » Blend underneath and onto neck.
	UNDEFINED CHEEKBONES	**TO GIVE CHEEKBONES MORE DIMENSION:** » Apply highlighter over very top of cheekbone. » Contour the hollow under cheekbone where cheekbones naturally indent. You may also use this technique to create a more dramatic emphasis for already well-defined cheekbones. Avoid creating obvious stripes of contour in an effort to create the illusion.
	RECEDING CHIN	**TO "BRING OUT" A CHIN THAT RECEDES:** » Apply highlighter on and under chin.

	POINTED CHIN	**TO MINIMIZE A POINTED CHIN:** » Contour with a slightly darker color.
	"DOUBLE" CHIN	**TO MAKE A "DOUBLE" CHIN RECEDE AND APPEAR SLIMMER:** » Contour heavier area with a darker color.
	BROAD OR SQUARE JAW	**TO MINIMIZE WIDTH IN THE JAW:** » Contour with a darker color along jaw and through sides of face. » You may use a deeper foundation than on the rest of the face to help create balance between upper and lower parts of face.
	HIGH OR BROAD FOREHEAD	**TO VISUALLY SHORTEN A HIGH FOREHEAD:** » Contour along outside edges or along top to narrow forehead.

EYES

The eyes, often called the windows to the soul, can be the most expressive feature of the face. Many first impressions are based on how well confidence and trust are communicated with the eyes. Since the eyes are such an attention-getting and important feature, you should be sure to use cosmetic artistry wisely in this area.

The three areas of the eye are the:
» Eyelid

» Crease area

» Brow bone

An eye that is in "perfect" or ideal proportions would have the following characteristics:
» Area between the base of the lashes and the crease line makes up one-third of the eye.

» Area between the crease line and the eyebrow makes up the remaining two-thirds.

» Well-spaced eyes have the width of one eye between them.

» "Close-set" eyes have a space of less than one eye between them.

» "Wide-set" eyes have a space greater than one eye between them.

Eyebrows

Brow design and the placement of lights and darks can visually alter the position of the eyes on the face. Notice how the eyes are actually the same distance apart in each of the three sets of eyes below.

Well-spaced eyes:
» Begin eyebrows at inside corner of eyes.
» Balance deeper tones across eyelid of eyes.

To make eyes appear close-set:
» Extend eyebrows beyond inside corner of eyes.
» Apply deeper tones toward inside of eyes.

To make eyes appear wide-set:
» Widen distance between brows.
» Apply deeper tones toward outside of eyes.

You can use the shape of the eyebrows to offset imperfections of other facial features. For example, straighter, more horizontal brows with a minimal arch will help diminish the illusion of length in a long face.

DISCOVER**MORE**

Brow Design
Trends in eyebrow designs are ever changing and unique to every individual. Personal preference also plays a role in the shape and design of eyebrows. The advantage of designing eyebrows with makeup is that it's not permanent; it can be removed and reapplied. Making mistakes is the best way to learn. Research eyebrow designs online.

Eye Shapes

The eyes can be visually altered by contouring and highlighting specific areas to achieve the desired eye shape.

	ALMOND EYES	**TO ENHANCE ALMOND EYES:** » Define natural shape with a smudgy eyeliner application over entire upper and lower lids. » Apply neutral shadow on lids into natural crease to add structure.
	SMALL EYES	**TO ENHANCE SMALL EYES:** » Brighter colors and soft shading of upper and lower lids help define eyes without closing them off. » Contouring above natural eyelid crease to leave eyelid free of shading creates an open, spacious feeling.
	WIDE-SET EYES	**TO MAKE WIDE-SET EYES APPEAR CLOSER TOGETHER:** » Apply shadows and eyeliners near inner corners of eyes. » Softly blend toward bridge of nose. This gives the illusion of pulling the eyes closer to the center of the face.
	CLOSE-SET EYES	**TO MAKE CLOSE-SET EYES APPEAR WIDER:** » Apply eyeliner to outer edges of top and bottom lids and extend lines outward. » Leave inner corners void of heavy color to create a lighter and brighter area with illusion of space. » Extending outer edges of eyebrows is also helpful.
	DEEP-SET EYES	**TO BRING FORWARD DEEP-SET EYES:** » Apply light and bright shadows to help bring area forward. » Eyeliners rich in color also add definition.
	BULGING EYES	**TO MAKE BULGING EYES APPEAR FLATTER:** » Apply deeper colors to contour protruding lid. » Lower lids and tops of eyelids can be lined with a deep eyeliner of same color, then connected at inner corners. » Shadow can then be "graded" from dark at lids to light as you approach brow bone. » Shadows can be blended in horizontal fashion to achieve a flattened appearance.

LIPS

Lips, like eyes, deserve special makeup considerations. Generally, a soft, natural look in lip color application is preferred, especially for daytime. You can use the principles of contouring and highlighting, using darker and lighter colors, to make "corrections" on different lip shapes. Remember to keep corrections as subtle and natural as possible to avoid an overly "drawn-on" look. Foundation should be applied to the lips prior to corrective lining.

		FULL TOP LIP	**TO MINIMIZE FULL TOP LIP:** » Line upper lip slightly inside natural shape, as shown by dotted line.
		FULL BOTTOM LIP	**TO MINIMIZE FULL BOTTOM LIP:** » Create a lower lipline within natural lipline. » Choose darker, more muted lip color. **TO MAKE TOP LIP FULLER:** » Leave upper lip unlined or line it slightly outside natural lipline. » Use a shade or two lighter lip color. » Be sure to use colors in same color family.
		FULL LIPS	**TO MINIMIZE FULL LIPS:** » Outline just inside natural lipline. » Choosing darker, more muted lip colors. » Blend carefully within "new" lipline.
		UNEVEN LIPS	**TO CREATE A MORE BALANCED LIP SHAPE:** » Apply lipliner to build up areas that are not large enough or defined enough.
		THIN LIPS	**TO MAKE THIN LIPS FULLER:** » Use brighter, lighter colors. » Outline just outside natural upper and lower lipline with a soft, curving line. **THIN LOWER LIP:** » Extend curve of lower lip to balance shape of mouth. **THIN UPPER LIP:** » Build up curve of upper lip to balance shape of mouth.

		SMALL MOUTH	TO MAKE SMALL MOUTH LARGER: » Build outside edges of upper and lower lips. » Line slightly outside natural lipline. » Extend corners of mouth outward.
		SHARPLY DEFINED "CUPID'S BOW"	TO MINIMIZE DEFINED "CUPID'S BOW": » Line upper lip by rounding off sharp peaks and widen curve of upper lip.
		DOWNTURNED LIPS	TO INVERT DOWNTURNED LIPS: » Create line that extends just above natural fall of lips on outer corners.

LESSONS LEARNED

Color theory presents three colors that are pure—red, yellow and blue—and then shows how primary and secondary colors can be mixed to produce various color options on a color wheel. Color schemes identify various color patterns that can be used to enhance client makeup designs. Patterns include:

» Monochromatic (same color)

» Analogous (three adjacent colors on the color wheel)

» Triadic (three colors in a triangular position on the color wheel)

» Complementary (colors across from each other on the color wheel)

» Warm and cool colors (tones found in skin colors and cosmetic colors)

The seven basic face shapes and the steps used to create the illusion of an oval shape are:

» Oval – Doesn't require much "corrective" application

» Round – Contour to slenderize and add vertical emphasis to appear more oval

» Square – Contour to soften the angularity and reduce the width

» Oblong – Visually shorten the face by contouring under the chin and horizontally at the hairline; add visual width when possible

» Pear – Highlight the forehead to add visual width; contour the bottom of the face to reduce width

» Diamond – Highlight the jaw and forehead to add visual width; contour the cheekbones to minimize the width

» Heart – Widen the jawline with highlighting; contour across the forehead to minimize width

It's the placement of light and dark colors that allow you to create the illusion of the desired nose, cheekbones, chin, forehead, eyebrows, eye shape and lips.

112.11 MAKEUP PRODUCTS AND DESIGN

EXPLORE //

How many makeup products do you own?

INSPIRE //

With the knowledge of makeup products and makeup design, you'll be able to create makeup designs for any occasion.

ACHIEVE //

Following this lesson on *Makeup Products and Design,* you'll be able to:

>> Identify the products used to create makeup designs

>> List the most common applications related to makeup design

FOCUS //

MAKEUP PRODUCTS AND DESIGN

Makeup Products

Makeup Design

112.11 | MAKEUP PRODUCTS AND DESIGN

Every makeup artist has a kit filled with an array of products to create a multitude of makeup designs. Knowing which product to use—and when—will help build your knowledge of the basics of makeup products and makeup design. Makeup designs are often categorized into Day, Evening and Special Occasion, such as Bridal.

MAKEUP PRODUCTS

The foundation for all makeup design begins with learning about basic products. Every product line will have unique characteristics, but are classified according to the area of the face they are designed to enhance. As you work with different product lines, you will begin to develop your own preferences based on colors and textures as well as current styles and fashion trends. Your choices will also depend on your clients' needs and the type of makeup design you are creating. The basis for all makeup design begins with the following products:

AREA	PRODUCTS	USE
SKIN	» Foundation » Concealer » Powder	Even out skin tone
EYES	» Eyebrows » Eye shadow » Eyeliner » Mascara	Enhance and define eyes
CHEEKS	» Blush » Bronzer	Add color to the face
LIPS	» Lipliner » Lip color	Enhance and define lips

SKIN PREPARATION

Before beginning any makeup application, you will need to prepare the client's skin. **Preparing the skin involves cleansing, toning, moisturizing and protecting the skin**. Creating a clean, smooth canvas to work on will ensure a smooth application and better product adherence. Refer to the lesson on *Skin Care* for the skin care regimen.

SKIN

With makeup design, it's important to create an even skin tone. There are several products that will help you achieve this, including concealer, foundation and facial powder.

SKIN COLOR CLASSIFICATIONS

TONE	SKIN COLOR	TONE	SKIN COLOR
LIGHT CREAMY	Yellow to slightly peach; light	OLIVE	Yellowish-green; medium to dark
GOLDEN	Yellow cast; light	BROWN	Usually olive-toned; medium to dark with red or yellow undertones
PINK	Pink or blue to red; light to medium	EBONY	Mahogany and/or blue undertones; dark to very dark
TAN	Caramel-colored to brown; light to dark with red or yellow undertones		

CONCEALER

Every makeup artist knows the necessity of correcting particular facial imperfections. You'll need to assess the skin for tone and value, as well as for specific problems. Problems such as under-eye circles (often with blue or purple undertones), broken capillaries and blemishes can and should be corrected. If they are not, they may stand out or detract from the completed makeup design.

Types of concealers include liquid, cream and stick. Liquid is used for light to medium coverage, cream is used for medium to heavy coverage and stick offers the heaviest coverage.

IF SKIN UNDERTONE IS:	USE A CONCEALER THAT HAS A:
YELLOW	VIOLET BASE
RED	GREEN BASE
GREEN	RED BASE
BLUE/PURPLE	YELLOW/ORANGE BASE

FOUNDATION

Foundation may be considered the most important makeup product. Today, many foundations also contain sunscreens, which can help protect skin from UV damage. Foundations are available in several forms including powder/mineral, liquid, cream, and pancake or pan-stick or grease-based.

Powder/mineral is a combination of makeup base and powder, called "one-step" or "dual finish." Additional powder may not be required. It creates a lighter, more natural effect and is good for sensitive skin.

Liquid is the most common form and provides a coverage with a natural appearance.

Cream has a heavier consistency than liquid and is used for additional coverage. Cream requires more careful blending than liquid.

Pancake (or pan-stick or grease-based) provides maximum coverage and is applied with water and a sponge. This form is used for photography and theater and/or for major corrections such as covering scars, large birthmarks or tattoos.

> When used for coverage, foundation:

- Evens out skin color and creates a smoother skin texture

- Provides a good canvas on which to create a makeup design

> When used for correction, foundation:

- Corrects undesirable skin tones such as sallowness or redness

- Conceals imperfections in the skin such as dilated blood vessels, freckles, birthmarks or blemishes

> **To test a foundation shade to determine if you have chosen the correct color, blend a small amount of foundation on the client's jawline.** The correct color will "disappear" into the client's skin. Unless correction is required, match the foundation to the skin tone to avoid any lines of demarcation.

FACIAL POWDER

Facial powders are primarily designed to "set" other makeup products so that they last longer without fading, streaking or rubbing off. **The most common forms are loose and pressed powders which are available in translucent and tinted shades.**

A colorless, translucent facial powder may be worn with any foundation shade, since it is designed to allow the skin/foundation shade to show through without imparting any color.

Tinted powders should be used in coordination with matching foundations and may also be worn successfully by clients who do not wear foundation and want only the sheerest coverage.

» Translucent powder is applied before powdered blushes or contour colors and can be applied after liquid or cream products, such as foundations or blushes.

» For tinted shades, application is with a powder brush, or large dome brush, which will yield lighter coverage. For heavier coverage, use a sponge or powder puff.

» Facial powder is generally applied before mascara.

If you are preparing your client for a special occasion, avoid facial waxing to prevent redness or irritation prior to the makeup application.

CONTOURING AND HIGHLIGHTING

Many cosmetic products can be used to contour and highlight the face. The most common products are:

Powder:

» Matte finish

» Best on oily skin types

» Applied with a brush

Liquid and creams:

» "Glowing" finish

» Best on dryer skin types

» Applied with a brush or sponge

Lighter shades of foundation are used to highlight a facial feature and darker shades of foundation are used to recess a facial feature. Blend highlighting and contouring well to achieve a subtle effect.

DISCOVER**MORE**

Was She Airbrushed?

Airbrushing makeup is an alternative to traditional makeup application. An airbrush gun is used to spray liquid makeup onto the skin. The mixture of air and makeup creates a very fine mist that creates a flawless appearance with a longevity of 12-24 hours. Airbrushing can be used for bridal to avant-garde makeup and can be used to apply foundation, eye color and cheek color. Go online and check out all the benefits of airbrushing and learn new skills and techniques.

EYES

Eyebrows "frame" the eyes and are very important to the balance of any face and makeup design. Whether the brows are natural or have been shaped, it may be necessary to shade or fill in to create the most attractive and flattering shape. The elements of eye design include eyebrow pencil, eyeliner, eye shadow, mascara and artificial lashes. Refer to the *Hair Removal* lesson for complete procedures on how to shape a well-arched eyebrow.

EYEBROW COLOR

Used to shade or fill in the brows. Keep the natural shape of the brow in mind, as it relates to the client's brow bone. Extreme changes in brow shape are appropriate for high-fashion and theatrical looks. Eyebrow colors come in pencil and powder.

>> Work with sharp pencils and use small, hair-like strokes.

>> Use two colors to give you a more natural effect and allow you to match hair color more closely.

>> Make sure you've filled the brow evenly, leaving no sparse areas.

>> Use a brow brush to soften the edges of the eyebrow.

>> Strive for symmetry as you work on the other eyebrow.

EYELINER

Eyeliner is used in makeup application to define and emphasize the shape and size of the eyes. Eyeliner is usually applied at the lash line. Eyeliners come in liquid, pencil and powder.

>> Liquids and powders are usually applied with a brush.

>> Pencil liners are applied to the eye using very short strokes.

>> Keep in mind that harder lines, such as those achieved with liquid liner, may not be as flattering and are generally reserved for evening or specific fashion makeup designs.

>> Pencil liners can be applied inside the eyelid (waterline), but be sure not to cover the tear duct since this may cause injury.

EYE SHADOW

Eye shadow is used to contour or highlight the eye. It is often the focal point of a complete makeup design, so you should carefully analyze the client's lifestyle and personality, as well as the occasion for which the makeup is being designed. Blending is especially crucial in this area, since colors are often more intense. Eye shadows come in many forms including creams, gel, powders, pencils or crayons

Shadows can:

>> Create a more contoured or exaggerated effect in areas such as the crease.

>> Highlight and accentuate areas such as the brow bone.

MASCARA

Mascara defines, lengthens and thickens the eyelashes. The depth of color used may also serve to enhance and bring out the eye shadow color used. Mascara is available in liquid, cake and cream forms.

>> Applied with disposable mascara wands and is generally applied to the upper and lower lashes.

>> Note that an eyelash curler may be used prior to the application of mascara to open up the eyes.

>> Use a lash separator after applying mascara to avoid a clumpy look.

ARTIFICIAL LASHES – OPTIONAL

Artificial lashes add length and fullness to natural lashes to create a dramatic effect. The most common artificial eyelash is the strip eyelash. These bands of lashes are applied along the natural lash line with adhesive. They are generally worn with evening makeup. The exception would be for individuals who have lost their lashes or have particularly sparse lashes.

Some clients might be allergic to an eyelash adhesive. As a precaution, perform a predisposition or allergy test first. Place a small amount of adhesive on the skin. If no adverse reaction occurs within 24 hours, you can safely use that adhesive on the client.

Application of Artificial Strip Lashes

Quality, human-hair lashes are the most natural looking. Brown or black will coordinate well enough to be worn with most hair colors. To apply artificial lashes, you will need an appropriate set of lashes, tweezers, scissors and lash adhesive. Follow these general steps to apply:

1. Begin by measuring the upper lash. Start midway between the inside corner of the eye and the curve where the iris begins and measure to the outside corner. If the lash is too long, trim it to fit.

2. Use your fingers to bend the lashes into a horseshoe shape to make them more flexible and easier to fit to the curve of the eyelid.

3. Apply a thin strip (small amount) of eyelash adhesive to the base of the artificial lashes and allow it to set for a few seconds.

4. Apply the lashes. Begin with the shorter, or inside, lashes and position them midway between the inside corner of the eye and the curve where the iris begins. Position the remaining lashes as close to the client's own lashes as possible. You may also work from the outside corner toward the inside corner, as long as the lashes have been accurately measured and trimmed.

5. Apply bottom lashes by using lash adhesive in the same manner as for the upper lashes. Place the lashes under the client's lower lashes, with shorter lashes toward the center of the eye and longer lashes toward the outside.

Eye tabs are another type of artificial eyelash. These are individual clusters of false lashes. Tabbing involves gluing these clusters along the natural lash line. These lashes will stay in place for several days before falling out. Research the pros and cons of tabbing before offering this service.

Eyelash extensions are individual lashes applied to the client's own lashes with specially designed adhesives, one or two lashes at a time. These extensions last until the natural lash falls out, approximately 6-8 weeks later. Clients return to the salon to fill in the lost lashes as needed. Eyelash extensions are a specialty service that may take a few hours and requires additional training and certification. Passing an Eyelash Extension licensure exam may be required by your regulatory agency before you can offer this service to clients.

CHEEKS

Maybe you've heard the expression "high cheekbones" before. What does that actually mean? Usually having high cheekbones means that the widest part of the face is just beneath the eyes, causing the cheek to indent slightly beneath the bone. This indent causes a slight shadow, which leads to accentuating the cheekbones, making them to appear "higher." The elements of cheek design include blush and bronzer.

BLUSH

Blush is used to add color to the face, especially to the cheek area. Without blush, the face may appear to be flat or dull, since foundation has evened out skin tone and reduced any natural "blush." Blush can also be used to enhance facial contouring. There are four types of blushes available: liquid, cream, gel and powder.

>> Liquid, cream and gel products are applied prior to the application of facial powder, usually with a small sponge. Powdered blush is applied after facial powder, usually with a brush.

>> **Liquid cheek color products seem to be suitable for all skin types.**

>> The fairness or darkness of your client's skin will determine the depth of the blush color you recommend. Blush should coordinate with the tones of the rest of the makeup application.

■ Warm eye makeup and lip colors require warmer blush colors.

■ Cooler makeup design requires a cooler blush color.

>> Blush color is generally applied for a soft or subtle effect. Apply in a C-shaped motion from the temple to the cheekbone, being careful not to extend beyond the middle of the eye.

>> If blush has been applied too heavily, soften the effect by applying translucent powder over it.

>> Like many other aspects of makeup design, blush application, particularly placement of color, will follow fashion trends. Be sure the application you choose is the most flattering to your client and not just the fad of the moment.

BRONZER

Like blush, bronzer is used to impart color onto the cheek area. It can give the illusion of tanned skin without the harmful rays of the sun.

>> Bronzer can also be used to contour areas of the face.

LIPS

The mouth should not "stand out" above the other facial features. Fashion trends may call for a stronger mouth at certain times, but overall, the makeup design should remain proportionally balanced. The elements of lip design include lipliner and lip color.

LIPLINER

Lipliner is applied to the outer edge of the lips to define the shape of the lips and to prevent lipstick from "bleeding" onto the skin around the mouth.

» Serves as a guideline for lips

» Used to visually correct imperfections in lip shape

» Prolongs the wear of any lip color

» Warm up the liner by drawing on the back of your hand or by rubbing the tip of the pencil between your thumb and index finger; this will allow it to go on more smoothly

LIP COLOR

The purpose of lip color is to complete the balance of color. It is usually the last cosmetic to be applied. Lipstick and lipliner can correct the shape and size of a mouth to make it more proportionate with the rest of the facial features. Lip color is available in a variety of forms, but primarily as lipstick and lip gloss.

» Lipstick:
  ■ Most common form
  ■ Contained in a cylindrical tube
  ■ Lipstick is best applied with a lip brush, which allows the contour of the mouth to be carefully followed or reshaped as needed

» Lip gloss:
  ■ Can be used as a highlighter over a lipstick shade, usually has moisturizing properties and is soothing for dry, chapped lips
  ■ Imparts a shiny appearance
  ■ Less concentration of color than lipsticks
  ■ Popular with younger girls who want some color, but not as much as a lipstick

» **Be cautious that the lip color you choose does not overpower the amount of color that you have applied to the cheeks and eyes.**

» Some lip products contain sunscreens to block out UV rays and prevent the lips from becoming chapped.

» As with all other makeup products, it is a good idea to look at the ingredients of lip color products, as well as the color, before making your selection.

LIP SHAPES

An examination of the ideal mouth and lips would reveal:

>> A frontal view in which the bottom lip is slightly fuller than the top, with a total shape and size that create balance and harmony with the rest of the facial features.

>> A side view that shows an indentation above the upper lip and below the bottom lip. The top lip, the bottom lip and the chin should extend forward almost equally.

SALONCONNECTION

Lights, Camera, Action!

Proper lighting is essential for any makeup application. Whether it be day, evening or bridal makeup, make sure to consider the lighting in which the makeup will be seen, and make adjustments according to the light in which you are working. Fluorescent lighting is composed of blue and green light and can be deceiving as it often accentuates blue or green undertones and cancels out warmer tones. Incandescent lighting is composed of red and yellow light. A combination of the two, therefore, is ideal for makeup applications because it is closest to natural light. If you are not working with this lighting combination, you may want to check your work by taking your client outside or close to a window. Remember also that since evening makeup tends to be more dramatic, you need to compensate when working under salon lighting or daylight.

MAKEUP DESIGN

Different occasions call for different makeup applications. Day, evening and bridal are just a few examples. The following is an overview of the areas of the face and what products are used in creating makeup designs.

DAY MAKEUP DESIGN

A day makeup application is generally more natural in appearance. It is meant to enhance the client's natural beauty without looking overly made up. It is not the number of products that you apply to the face, it's the application of the products that matters. The application of day makeup is outlined below. Refer to the *Day Makeup Workshop* for complete step-by-step application. Note that the order of product application can vary.

First, you'll want to prepare the client's skin. Then assess the skin, tone and value, as well as looking for specific problems. To match the foundation to the skin tone, you'll need to test it along the client's jawline on to the neck. The correct foundation shade will "disappear" into the skin. Note that the skin on the neck is generally lighter than the skin on the face. The best foundation choice is a balance between these two areas.

SKIN

Concealer

>> Remove small amount of product from container with spatula and transfer onto palate.

>> Apply concealer to face with camouflage brush to areas that tend to be dark or recessed, such as under and around eyes and sides of nostrils.

>> Blend with cosmetic sponge.

Remember to apply a minimal amount of pressure around the eyes to help maintain elasticity of the skin tissue and prevent wrinkling and creasing.

Foundation

>> Transfer a dime-size amount of product to palate.

>> Apply foundation to cheek area, forehead, nose and chin.

>> Blend product onto face with cosmetic sponge using a pat-and-roll motion called stippling.

>> Continue to blend each section toward hairline and neck.

>> Avoid any lines of demarcation.

You may choose to apply foundation to eyelids, earlobes and lips.

Powder

>> Apply powder using large powder brush or large dome brush.

>> Smooth powder over face using pat-and-roll motion.

>> Avoid applying powder to eyelids and eyelashes.

>> Remove any excess powder with a large, clean brush.

Facial powder is generally applied before mascara whereas liquid, cream or gel blush is usually applied prior to powder.

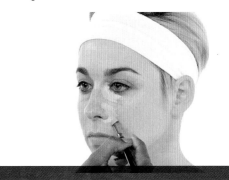

EYES

Eyebrows

>> Shade or fill in eyebrows using colored powder and brush or pencil.

>> Begin at inner corner of eyebrow.

>> Apply color using delicate, even strokes.

>> Work toward the peak of the arch and out to outside corner.

>> Clean and refine shape with cosmetic sponge.

>> Brush eyebrows using an upward motion to restore proper shape and remove excess product.

>> Check for symmetry.

Eyeliner

>> Sharpen eyeliner pencil and wipe with a tissue.

>> Lift eyelid upward using your thumb positioned under eyebrow.

>> Apply thin line along upper and lower lashline.

>> Use angle brush to blend and soften pencil line.

>> Check for symmetry.

Eye Shadow

>> Apply eye shadow to crease area using a patting motion.

>> Blend and soften with blending brush.

Remember to apply very little pressure to eye area to preserve and protect the delicate skin in this area.

Mascara

>> Coat a disposable wand with mascara.

>> Using your thumb, pull eyebrow up to lift eyelid slightly.

>> Place mascara wand horizontally along base of lashes.

>> Apply mascara by moving wand upward and outward from base to ends of lashes.

>> Use a clean wand to apply mascara to other eye.

>> Use an eyelash separator to separate and define lashes.

To curl eyelash prior to mascara application:
>> Position eyelashes in between pads of eyelash curler.

>> Gently close eyelash curler for a few seconds.

>> Open and release.

CHEEKS

Blush

>> Apply blush using a C-shaped motion from temple to cheekbone with a fan brush.

>> Do not exceed beyond the middle of eye.

>> If blush has been applied too heavily, soften the effect by applying translucent powder over it.

LIPS

Lipliner

>> Use lipliner (pencil) or lip brush to line the lips.

>> Start lining upper lip at outside corners and work from either side toward center or the "bow" of the lips.

>> Line lower lip from outside corner toward center.

>> Make any "corrections" in lip shape at this point.

>> Use a natural tone, two or three shades darker than the natural lip color or one that matches the tone of chosen lipstick.

Lip Color

>> Remove lip color from tube or container with spatula.

>> Transfer color onto sanatizible or disposable lip brush.

>> Use lip brush to fill the entire lip shape with lip color.

>> Blend to edge of lip shape, but not beyond lipliner.

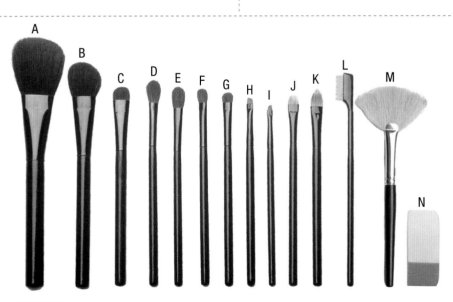

A. Large powder brush (dome)
B. Contoured brush
C. Medium chisel brush
D. Large blending brush
E. Medium fluff brush
F. Small fluff brush
G. Small chisel brush
H. Angle brush
I. Detail angle brush
J. Lip brush
K. Large camouflage brush
L. Eyelash separator
M. Fan brush
N. Latex sponge

BRUSHES

Many different brushes can be used to apply various makeup products. The brushes used to blend and contour are often chosen based on their size and shape. However, the size and shape of the area of application can also help determine which brushes are best to use. It is important to have a selection of makeup brushes available. Note that brush names may vary among manufacturers.

REMEMBER
Makeup applicators need to be discarded or disinfected after each use to follow infection control guidelines.

EVENING MAKEUP DESIGN

Many of the actual step-by-step techniques remain the same for an evening makeup application, however, there are distinct differences. Since evening makeup is seen in softer, more indirect lighting, intense colors are used to create more dramatic effects.

DAY MAKEUP DESIGN

EVENING MAKEUP DESIGN

EYES

>> Darker eyeliner can be used for more depth of color.

>> More intense eye shadow color can be used.

>> Apply with a dabbing motion for more intense concentration of color.

>> Color is contoured into the crease and slightly beyond for a dramatic effect.

>> Color is often "wrapped" around the eye for evening, bringing color and emphasis to the area below the eye.

>> Heavier eyeliner and mascara application can be used for more definition.

LIPS AND CHEEKS

>> Use darker colors for a stronger, more defined mouth.

>> Stronger eye and lip colors may require stronger cheek color, so carefully check the balance of the face.

DARK SKIN MAKEUP DESIGN

In general, darker skin can carry off more color than lighter skin colors without looking overly made-up. The step-by-step techniques are the same as day makeup with some notable differences seen below. Regardless of the pattern of application, richer, more intense colors can often be used on darker skin tones. Keep the overall balance of color in mind as you perform your makeup application. Note that the application shown here is an example of an evening look. Refer to the *Dark Skin Evening Makeup Workshop* to see a complete application.

SKIN

>> Foundations and concealers should be well chosen, as it is easy to go too light or too cool in your color choice.

>> Yellow-based products are often appropriate for darker skin colors. Concealers and foundations that are too cool will look ashy or gray.

EYES

>> A pencil will create a stronger, more defined brow than a powder.

CHEEKS

>> More cheek color may need to be applied in order to be effective.

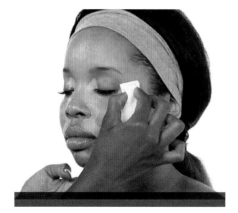

BRIDAL MAKEUP DESIGN

It's that once-in-a-lifetime occasion when a woman wants to look more beautiful than ever. Yet weddings and brides present special challenges to the professional makeup artist. Her makeup needs to last all day and/or evening with minimal upkeep. Many brides wear their hair up for their big day, and that can alter the appearance of the face shape. Brides usually wear white, ivory or other very light colors, which have the effect of draining color from faces with lighter skin tones.

One of the biggest challenges to the professional makeup artist is to create a makeup design that looks naturally beautiful to the naked eye and that can hold up to photography. Shown here are some specific points to consider when designing makeup for the bridal client. Ideally, the only touch-up products needed should be powder, lipliner and lipstick.

SKIN

>> Make sure that skin is well prepared—exfoliated earlier if needed. The "canvas" should be as perfect as possible. Make sure skin is moisturized, but not oily. This precaution is especially important around the eyes. Preparation ensures that the makeup design will look good and helps the makeup to last longer.

>> On oily skins, avoid face, cheek and eye products with orange or strong yellow undertones. These colors tend to oxidize more on oily skin and turn more yellow.

>> Remember that many types of photographic lighting have cool undertones and will bring out cool tones in the makeup design. Stay with a neutral-to-warmer palette.

>> Foundation should match and complement the bride's skin tone. Apply the least amount possible for a fresh, natural look. Use concealer on the inside corner of the eyes to hide imperfections.

>> Many gowns have lower-cut necklines. Be sure to powder the skin in the exposed areas so that light reflections in the face and the décolletage are similar.

>> An extra tip for "camera-ready" makeup: Be sure not to powder until after the eye makeup is complete. Then clean up under the eye using concealer on a latex sponge or small brush.

CHEEKS

>> For longer-lasting cheek color, apply a cream blush (if skin is not oily), followed by an application of powder blush after the face has been powdered.

EYES

>> Curl the lashes and use waterproof mascara.

>> Eyes and brows should be accentuated with definition more than with color. Brows tend to "disappear" in photographs, so make sure they are well groomed and defined.

LIPS

>> There is usually a bit of kissing going on at a wedding, so use good judgment in the design of lips. Avoid overly glossy products that may smear.

>> Use a long-lasting lipliner—products with silicone are excellent—and apply to the entire lip. Use a color about 2-3 shades darker than the natural lip color and that matches the tone of the lipstick color.

Your ability to apply the theory and techniques of professional makeup application will increase the number of services you can offer your clients.

LESSONS LEARNED

The types of products used to create a makeup design are classified according to where they are applied to the face:

>> Skin
   ■ Foundation, concealer, powder

>> Eyes
   ■ Eyebrows, eye shadow, eyeliner, mascara

>> Cheeks
   ■ Blush, bronzer

>> Lips
   ■ Lipliner and lip color

The most common applications related to makeup design are:

>> Day

>> Evening

>> Dark Skin

>> Bridal

112.12
MAKEUP
GUEST EXPERIENCE

EXPLORE //

Do you know people who won't leave the house without wearing makeup?

INSPIRE //

Being able to apply makeup creatively and knowledgeably to achieve specific visual results leads to satisfied clients and rewarding results for you as a professional.

ACHIEVE //

Following this lesson on *Makeup Guest Experience,* you'll be able to:

>> Identify the service essentials related to makeup

>> Provide examples of infection control and safety guidelines for makeup services

>> Explain the three areas of a makeup service

FOCUS //

MAKEUP GUEST EXPERIENCE

Makeup Service Essentials

Makeup Infection Control and Safety

Makeup Service Overview

Makeup Rubric

112.12 | MAKEUP GUEST EXPERIENCE

AMAKEUP SERVICE ESSENTIALS

As with all professional services, communicating with your client prior to the actual service will ensure predictable results and will help you avoid any misunderstandings that may arise. As you review the four makeup service essentials, remember the importance of active listening, critical thinking and analysis of the overall success of the service.

CONNECT

>> Meet and greet the client with a firm handshake and a pleasant tone of voice.

>> Communicate to build rapport and develop a relationship with the client.

>> Have client fill out a makeup service record form.

CONSULT

>> Ask questions to discover the purpose of the makeup application. Ask questions such as, "Is this for a special occasion?", or whether the client has come in for a makeup application lesson.

>> Analyze your client's skin tone and type.

>> Assess the facts and thoroughly think through your recommendations by visualizing the end result.

>> Explain your recommended face design and color selections, products and the price for today's service(s), as well as for future services.

>> Gain feedback from your client and obtain consent before proceeding with the service.

CREATE

>> Ensure client comfort during service.

>> Stay focused on delivering the service to the best of your ability.

>> If explanations are needed, be clear and precise.

COMPLETE

>> Request satisfaction feedback from your client.

>> Escort client to retail area and show products used during service.

>> Recommend products for future makeup applications.

>> Invite your client to make a purchase.

>> Ask your client for referrals for future services.

>> Suggest a future appointment time and offer to prebook your client's next visit.

>> Offer appreciation to your client for visiting the school or salon.

>> Record recommended products on client record for future visits.

MAKEUP INFECTION CONTROL AND SAFETY

It is your responsibility as a professional to protect your client by following infection control and safety guidelines with any and all services you provide.

Cleaning is a process of removing dirt, debris and potential pathogens to aid in slowing the growth of pathogens. Cleaning is performed prior to disinfection procedures.

Disinfection methods kill certain pathogens (bacteria, viruses and fungi) with the exception of spores. Disinfectants are available in varied forms, including concentrate, liquid, spray or wipes that are approved EPA-registered disinfectants available for use in the salon industry. Complete immersion and the use of disinfecting spray or wipes are the most often used practices when it comes to disinfecting tools, multi-use supplies and equipment in the salon. Be sure to follow the manufacturer's directions for mixing disinfecting solutions and contact time, if applicable.

CLEANING AND DISINFECTION GUIDELINES

Keep in mind that only nonporous tools, supplies and equipment can be disinfected. All single-use items must be discarded after each use. Always follow your area's regulatory guidelines.

TOOLS/SUPPLIES	FUNCTION	CLEANING GUIDELINES	DISINFECTION GUIDELINES
HEADBAND	» Holds client's hair out of the way during application	» Remove hair and debris. » Wash in washing machine after each use.	» Use an additive that disinfects wet linens.
COTTON	» Removes product	» Single use item; must be discarded.	» Cannot be disinfected.
TOWEL/MAKEUP DRAPE	» Protects client's clothing	» Wash in washing machine after each use. » Dry thoroughly.	» Use an approved laundry additive if required by area's regulatory agency.

TOOLS/SUPPLIES	FUNCTION	CLEANING GUIDELINES	DISINFECTION GUIDELINES
TISSUE	» Blots the skin » Removes excess product	» Single use item; must be discarded.	» Cannot be disinfected.
COTTON SWABS	» Clean up » Correct errors	» Single use item; must be discarded.	» Cannot be disinfected.
PALETTE	» Holds desired amount of product(s)	» Preclean with soap and water.	» Use an approved EPA-registered disinfectant; wipe or spray as directed.
SPATULAS	» Remove product(s) from containers	» Single use item; must be discarded.	» If multiple-use item, immerse in an approved EPA-registered disinfectant solution.
COSMETIC SPONGES	» Apply foundation and concealer; blending; clean up	» Single use item; must be discarded.	» Cannot be disinfected.
TWEEZERS	» Shape eyebrows » Remove stray hairs	» Remove hair and debris. » Preclean with soap and water.	» Immerse in an approved EPA-registered disinfectant solution.
BRUSHES	» Apply makeup » Specific to needs	» Preclean with soap and water.	» Use an EPA-registered brush cleaner disinfectant.

TOOLS/SUPPLIES	FUNCTION	CLEANING GUIDELINES	DISINFECTION GUIDELINES
EYELASH CURLER	» Curls and enhances lashes	» Preclean with soap and water.	» Immerse in an approved EPA-registered disinfectant solution.
DISPOSABLE MASCARA WANDS	» Apply mascara	» Single use item; must be discarded.	» Cannot be disinfected.
LIP BRUSHES	» Apply lip color	» Preclean with soap and water.	» Immerse in an approved EPA-registered disinfectant solution.
BROW BRUSH/ LASH SEPARATOR	» Separates lashes after mascara application » Combs eyebrows into shape	» Preclean with soap and water.	» Immerse in an approved EPA-registered disinfectant solution.

Store disinfected tools and multi-use supplies in a clean, dry, covered container or cabinet.

MAKEUP EQUIPMENT

The equipment that you use during the makeup application will serve to make your application easier, as well as deliver the desired look that the client wants to achieve. Equipment is disinfected by wiping it down with an approved EPA-registered disinfectant.

EQUIPMENT	FUNCTION	CLEANING GUIDELINES	DISINFECTION GUIDELINES
MIRROR	» Allows artist to check balance; allows client to follow application		» Use an approved EPA-registered disinfectant; wipe or spray as directed.
PROPER LIGHTING	» Allows artist to work accurately and gauge results	» Clean as recommended by manufacturer.	
MAKEUP CHAIR	» Places client at proper height for makeup application/service		» Use an approved EPA-registered disinfectant; wipe or spray as directed.

SALON**CONNECTION**

Increasing Makeup Services

Makeup clients love to be pampered! They may only be coming into the salon for a haircut, yet with the proper makeup products, staff and client education as well as in-salon promotions, a salon can successfully help clients look and feel great by promoting professional makeup services. Here are a few strategies to increase makeup services:

» Offer complimentary makeup touch-ups

» Feature guest makeup artists

» Offer tester samples

» Promote wedding party makeup services

» Share trends in makeup with email blasts

CARE AND SAFETY

Follow infection control procedures for personal care and client safety guidelines before and during the makeup design service to ensure your safety and the client's, while also contributing to the salon care.

Personal Care	Client Care Prior to the Service	Client Care During the Service	Salon Care
» Check that your personal standards of hygiene minimize the spread of infection.	» Seat client in comfortable position for the service.	» Be aware of any skin sensitivity.	» Follow health and safety guidelines, including cleaning and disinfecting procedures.
» Wash hands and dry thoroughly with a single-use towel.	» Use a fresh drape on every client.	» Remove product if you see signs of allergic reactions to the cosmetic products, such as redness, swelling or inflammation.	» Ensure equipment is clean and disinfected.
» Keep your fingernails well-groomed to avoid scratching your clients.	» Cleanse, tone, moisturize and protect the skin.	» Work carefully around nonremovable jewelry/ piercings.	» Promote a professional image by assuring your workstation is clean and tidy throughout the service.
» Disinfect workstation.	» Carefully read and follow manufacturer's instructions for tools, supplies, products and equipment.	» Avoid excess pressure in and around the eye area.	» Disinfect all tools after each use. Always use disinfected tools, supplies and equipment for each client.
» Clean and disinfect tools appropriately.	» Handle tools and products with care.	» Avoid using products and makeup directly from containers. » Use spatulas to place the desired amount of product on your makeup palette. If more product is needed, remember to use a fresh spatula.	» Use disposable applicators whenever possible and discard after use.
» Minimize fatigue by maintaining good posture during the service.	» If any tools are dropped be sure to pick them up, then clean and disinfect.	» Be aware of nonverbal cues the client may be conveying.	» Sharpen all pencils before and after each use.
» Refer to your area's regulatory agency for proper mixing or handling of disinfectant solutions.		» Place soiled towel(s) in appropriate covered receptacle.	
		» Exercise extra precautions to avoid getting products or tools in the eyes.	

MAKEUP PRODUCTS

Safety Data Sheets (SDS) for all products used in the salon should be easily available for your use.

PRODUCTS	FUNCTION
Cleanser/Makeup Remover	Removes dirt, makeup and impurities
Toner	Helps further cleanse, soothe and smooth the skin while bringing it to a normal pH
Moisturizer	Hydrates and protects the skin
Sunscreen	Protects client's skin from UV damage
Concealer	Eliminates discolorations; reduces appearance of blemishes
Foundation	Creates an even skin tone and uniform surface
Blush/Bronzer	Adds color or contour
Eyeliner	Accentuates and defines shape of eyes
Eye Shadow	Contours and highlights the eyes
Brow Pencil/Powder	Fills in; corrects shape of eyebrow
Mascara	Defines, lengthens and thickens the eyelashes
Lipliner	Defines natural or corrected shape of the lips
Lip Color	Adds color and texture to the lips

MAKEUP SERVICE OVERVIEW

The Makeup Service Overview identifies the Preparation, Procedure and Completion areas for all makeup services:

» The Makeup Preparation provides a brief overview of the steps to follow *before* you actually begin the makeup service.

» The Makeup Procedure provides an overview of the procedures that you will use *during* the makeup service to ensure predictable results.

» The Makeup Completion provides an overview of the steps to follow *after* performing the makeup service to ensure guest satisfaction.

MAKEUP SERVICE OVERVIEW

MAKEUP PREPARATION	>> Clean and disinfect workstation and makeup chair. >> Arrange disinfected make up tools and supplies including brushes, disposable applicators, spatula, headband and assorted makeup. >> Wash hands. >> Perform analysis of skin. >> Ask client to remove jewelry; store in a secure place.

MAKEUP PROCEDURE	>> Drape client for the service (including headband and positioning chair).
	>> Use disposable applicators whenever possible and discard after each use.
	>> Use spatula to remove products from containers.
	>> Sharpen all pencils before and after each use.
	>> Avoid excess pressure in and around eye area.
	>> Exercise extra precautions to avoid getting products or tools in the eyes.
	>> Prepare the skin:
	  ▪ Cleanse, tone, moisturize and protect.
	  ▪ Assess facial shape and skin tone.
	>> Groom brows (brush and/or tweeze).
	>> Select and apply appropriate foundation and concealer color.
	  ▪ Test foundation color along the client's jawline.
	  ▪ Apply and blend concealer as needed with minimal amount of pressure around eye area.
	  ▪ Foundation should blend into the hairline and to the neck, avoiding any lines of demarcation.
	>> Shade brows (brush and fill in as needed).
	>> Apply eye shadow, eyeliner and mascara:
	  ▪ Eye shadow is applied and blended properly.
	  ▪ Eyeliner is used to define and emphasize the shape and size of the eyes.
	  ▪ Mascara is applied to define, lengthen and thicken the eyelashes.
	  ▪ Applied with a disposable mascara wand
	>> Select blush color and apply to cheekbones:
	  ▪ Cream, liquid or gel blush is applied before facial powder (tinted or translucent).
	  ▪ Powder blush is applied after facial powder (tinted or translucent).
	>> Apply facial powder (tinted or translucent) to "set" other makeup products.
	>> Select and apply appropriate lip color:
	  ▪ Lipliner is applied to the outer edge of the lips to define the shape.
	  ▪ Lip color is applied to complete the balance of color.
	>> Check application for proper blending and overall symmetry.
	>> Remove product if signs of allergic reaction are visible (redness, swelling, inflammation).

MAKEUP COMPLETION	>> Reinforce client's satisfaction with overall experience. >> Make professional product recommendations. >> Prebook client's next appointment. >> End client's visit with warm and personal goodbye. >> Discard single-use supplies; disinfect tools and multi-use supplies; disinfect workstation and arrange in proper order. >> Complete client record. >> Wash hands.

MAKEUP RUBRIC

A performance rubric is a document that identifies defined criteria at which levels of performance can be measured objectively. The following rubric is an example that your instructor might choose to use for scoring. The Makeup Rubric is divided into three main areas—Preparation, Procedure, Completion. Each area is further divided into step-by-step procedures that will ensure client safety and satisfaction.

MAKEUP RUBRIC

Student Name:_____ ID Number: _____

Instructor: _____ Date: _____ Start Time: _____ End Time: _____

MAKEUP (Live Model) — *Each scoring item is marked with either a "Yes" or a "No." Each "Yes" counts for one point. Total number of points attainable is 35.*

CRITERIA	YES	NO	INSTRUCTOR ASSESSMENT
PREPARATION: *Did student…*			
1. Set up workstation with properly labeled supplies?	☐	☐	
2. Place disinfected tools and supplies at a visibly clean workstation?	☐	☐	
3. Wash hands?	☐	☐	
Connect: Did student…			
4. Meet and greet client with a welcoming smile and pleasant tone of voice?	☐	☐	
5. Communicate to build rapport and develop a relationship with client?	☐	☐	
6. Refer to client by name throughout service?	☐	☐	
Consult: Did student…			
7. Ask questions to discover client's wants and needs?	☐	☐	
8. Analyze client's skin and check for any contraindications?	☐	☐	
9. Gain feedback and consent from client before proceeding?	☐	☐	
PROCEDURE: *Did student…*			
10. Properly drape client and prepare for the service?	☐	☐	
11. Use spatula to remove products from container?	☐	☐	
Create: Did student…			
12. Cleanse, tone, moisturize and protect the client's skin?	☐	☐	
13. Groom brows (brush and/or tweeze)?	☐	☐	
14. Select appropriate concealer color?	☐	☐	
15. Apply and blend concealer color?	☐	☐	
16. Select appropriate foundation color?	☐	☐	
17. Apply foundation color with no lines of demarcation?	☐	☐	
18. Shade brows (brush and fill in as needed) symmetrically?	☐	☐	
19. Apply and blend eye shadow?	☐	☐	
20. Apply eyeliner to define and emphasize shape and size of eyes?	☐	☐	
21. Select and apply blush when appropriate (cream, liquid or gel; powder)?	☐	☐	
22. Select and apply facial powder (tinted or translucent) to set other makeup products?	☐	☐	
23. Apply mascara with a disposable wand?	☐	☐	
24. Select and apply appropriate lipliner to define the shape?	☐	☐	
25. Apply lip color to complete the balance of color?	☐	☐	
26. Ensure makeup application is blended and balanced?	☐	☐	
COMPLETION *(Complete):* Did student…			
27. Ask questions and look for verbal and nonverbal cues to determine client's level of satisfaction?	☐	☐	
28. Make professional product recommendations?	☐	☐	
29. Ask client to make a future appointment?	☐	☐	
30. End guest's visit with a warm and personal goodbye?	☐	☐	
31. Discard single-use supplies?	☐	☐	
32. Disinfect tools and multi-use supplies; disinfect workstation and arrange in proper order?	☐	☐	
33. Complete service within scheduled time?	☐	☐	
34. Complete client record?	☐	☐	
35. Wash their hands following service?	☐	☐	

COMMENTS: _____   TOTAL POINTS = _____ ÷ 35 = _____ %

LESSONS LEARNED

>> The service essentials related to makeup include:

- Connect – To build rapport

- Consult – To ask questions, analyze skin tone and type, assess the facts, explain the plan and gain feedback

- Create – To deliver the service to the best of your ability

- Complete – To request satisfaction feedback, recommend retail products, ask for purchase, referrals, future appointment, offer appreciation and complete client record

>> Examples of infection control and safety guidelines for makeup services include:

- Carefully read and follow manufacturer's instructions for tools, supplies, products and equipment.

- Use a fresh drape on every client.

- Use spatulas to place the desired amount of product on your makeup palette. If more product is needed, remember to use a fresh spatula.

- Store soiled towels in an appropriate covered receptacle until laundered.

- Ensure equipment is clean and disinfected.

- Use disposable applicators whenever possible and discard after use.

- Sharpen all pencils before and after each use.

>> The three areas of a makeup service could be explained as:

- Preparation – Prepare the workstation, tools and supplies, wash your hands, perform analysis of skin and ask client to remove jewelry

- Procedure – Drape client; prepare the skin; groom the brows; select and apply foundation and concealer, shade brows; apply eye shadow, eyeliner and mascara; select and apply blush color to cheek bones; apply facial powder; select and apply lip color; check blending and overall symmetry

- Completion – Request satisfaction feedback; recommend retail products, ask for purchase, referrals, future appointment, offer a warm and personal goodbye; discard single-use supplies; disinfect tools and multi-use supplies; disinfect workstation and arrange in proper order; complete client record; wash hands

DAY MAKEUP

EXPLORE

Why do you think so many people watch makeup tutorials on YouTube?

INSPIRE

From everyday to avant-garde, from Broadway to bridal, the application of makeup all begins with the basic steps.

ACHIEVE

Following this *Day Makeup Workshop*, you'll be able to:

>> Demonstrate the steps used during a day makeup design

PERFORMANCE GUIDE

PERFORMANCE GUIDE

DAY MAKEUP

View the video, then perform this workshop. Complete the self-check as you progress through the workshop.

30 mins
Suggested
Salon Speed

PREPARATION	✔

>> Assemble tools, supplies and products
>> Set up workstation
>> Wash your hands

☐

CLIENT/SKIN PREPARATION	

1. **Cleanse, tone, moisturize and protect skin:**

>> Cleanse skin to remove any residual makeup
>> Use toner to restore pH
>> Apply moisturizer
>> Use sunscreen to protect skin

☐

2. **Analyze skin and facial features:**

>> Determine skin tone
>> Determine type of skin (normal, dry, oily, combination)
>> Assess face, eyebrow, eye and lip shapes

☐

3. **Drape client and position headband at hairline to keep hair off face.**

☐

	✔

4. Groom eyebrows if needed:

>> Brush eyebrows
>> Shape eyebrows following general guidelines
■ Begin on inside corner of eye
■ Peak occurs over outside iris of eye
■ End at outside of eye
>> Tweeze if required

FACE – CONCEALER AND FOUNDATION

5. Select concealer and foundation color:

>> Test color along jawline

6. Apply concealer with camouflage brush to areas that have shadows or discolorations:

>> Form half-moon shape over inside corner of both eyes
>> Create triangular shape around both sides of nasal fold
>> Blend with sponge
>> Apply under both eyes close to lashline
>> Blend eye area toward bridge of nose
>> Use minimal pressure

7. Apply foundation with camouflage brush to cheek area, forehead, nose and chin.

8. Blend foundation with sponge using stippling technique:

>> Blend each section outward before moving on
>> Use gentle pressure; too much pressure can result in broken capillaries
>> Color should blend or fade away into hairline and neck
>> Avoid any lines of demarcation

Note: Remember to include foundation color on the earlobes and lips.

EYES — EYELINER AND EYE SHADOW   ✔

Optional: Apply and blend shadow primer or base to eyelid prior to color application.

9. **Shade or fill in eyebrows using colored powder and brush or pencil:**
   - >> Begin on inside corner of eye
   - >> Work toward peak of arch
   - >> Narrow shape of eyebrow toward outside corner
   - >> Use small hair-like strokes
   - >> Use sponge to clean and refine line of brow
   - >> Brush both brows
   - >> Check for symmetry

10. **Apply eyeliner to upper and lower lashline:**
   - >> Lift eyelid upward using thumb positioned under eyebrow
   - >> Use short strokes from center of lashline outward
   - >> Use detail angle brush to soften and blend line
   - >> Check for symmetry

11. **Apply eye shadow to crease area using a patting motion:**
   - >> Blend and soften eye shadow with blending brush
   - >> Use very little pressure to protect eye area

   Note: Eye shadow can also be applied prior to eyeliner.

FACE – FACIAL POWDER

12. **Apply tinted or translucent facial powder throughout face and neck using large powder brush:**
    - ›› Smooth powder over face using pat-and-roll motion
    - ›› Avoid eyelids and eyelashes

EYES – MASCARA

Optional: An eyelash curler may be used prior to application of mascara:
- ›› Position eyelashes in between eyelash curler pads
- ›› Gently close the eyelash curler for a few seconds
- ›› Open and release

13. **Apply mascara with disposable mascara wand:**
    - ›› Hold eyelid upward and instruct client to look down
    - ›› Place wand horizontally along base of lashes
    - ›› Move wand upward and outward from base to ends of lashes
    - ›› Use an eyelash separator to separate and define lashes

CHEEKS – BLUSH

14. **Apply powder blush using a C-shaped motion from temple to cheekbone with fan brush.**

    Note: Cream, liquid or gel blush is applied prior to facial powder. Blush may be applied prior to mascara.

LIPS – LIP COLOR ✔

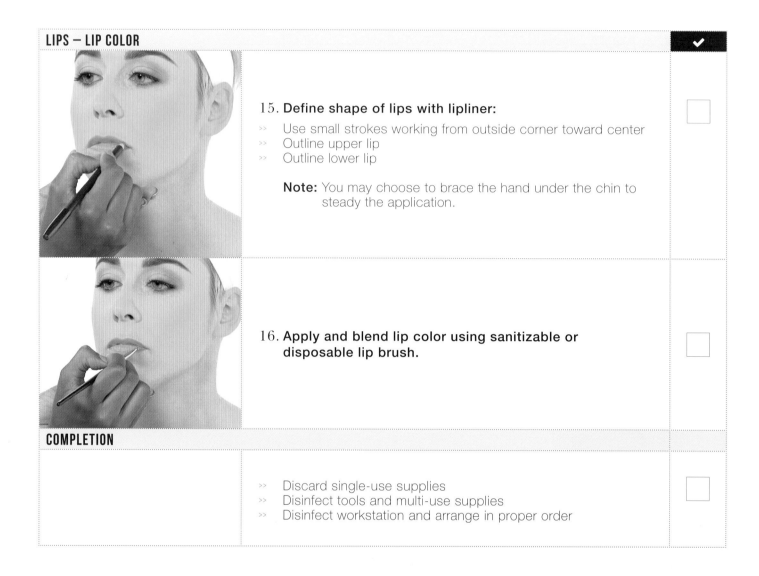

15. **Define shape of lips with lipliner:**
    >> Use small strokes working from outside corner toward center
    >> Outline upper lip
    >> Outline lower lip

    Note: You may choose to brace the hand under the chin to steady the application.

16. **Apply and blend lip color using sanitizable or disposable lip brush.**

COMPLETION

>> Discard single-use supplies
>> Disinfect tools and multi-use supplies
>> Disinfect workstation and arrange in proper order

30 mins
Suggested Salon Speed

My Speed
_____
_____
_____

INSTRUCTIONS:

Record your time in comparison with the suggested salon speed. Then, list here how you could improve your performance.

_____
_____
_____
_____
_____

EVENING MAKEUP

EXPLORE

Why do you think women choose to wear strong makeup colors at night?

INSPIRE

Learning evening makeup techniques will increase your knowledge of makeup design.

ACHIEVE

Following this *Evening Makeup Workshop*, you'll be able to:

>> Demonstrate proper procedures to perform an evening makeup design

EVENING MAKEUP

View the video, then perform this workshop. Complete the self-check as you progress through the workshop.

30 mins
Suggested
Salon Speed

PREPARATION	✔
>> Assemble tools, supplies and products >> Set up workstation >> Wash your hands	☐

SKIN PREPARATION

1. Cleanse, tone, moisturize and protect skin. ☐

2. Analyze skin and facial features. ☐

3. Drape client and position head band. ☐

4. Groom brows if needed. ☐

5. Select concealer and foundation color. ☐

6. Apply and blend concealer. ☐

7. Apply and blend foundation. ☐

8. Shade or fill in eyebrows. ☐

   Note: Refer to *Day Makeup Workshop* for steps 1-8.

EYES — EYELINER AND EYE SHADOW

9. Apply darker eyeliner along entire upper lashline for more depth of color: ☐
   >> Use small strokes

10. Repeat eyeliner application on opposite eye. ☐

11. Blend eyeliner on both eyes with small detail brush:

>> Balance both eyes

12. Apply darker eye shadow color using dabbing technique to achieve a more intense concentration of color.

13. Blend eye shadow upward with brush:

>> Contour in the crease and slightly beyond for more dramatic effect
>> Avoid harsh line
>> Check for symmetry

14. Extend darker eye shadow color under eyes to add emphasis.

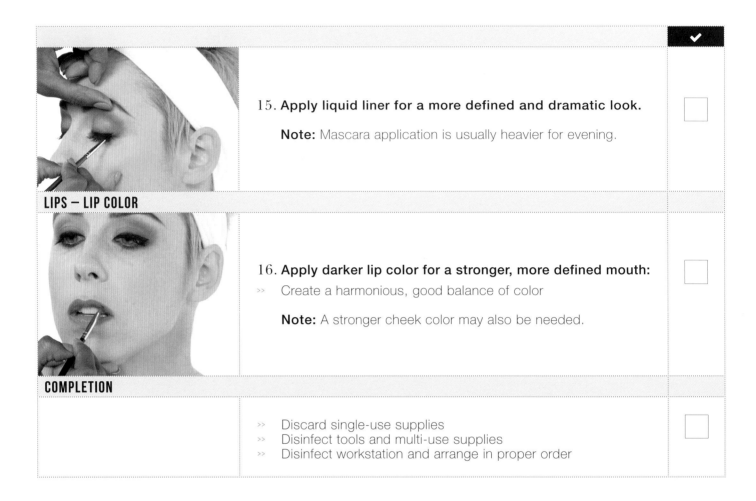

15. Apply liquid liner for a more defined and dramatic look.

    Note: Mascara application is usually heavier for evening.

LIPS – LIP COLOR

16. Apply darker lip color for a stronger, more defined mouth:

>> Create a harmonious, good balance of color

    Note: A stronger cheek color may also be needed.

COMPLETION

>> Discard single-use supplies
>> Disinfect tools and multi-use supplies
>> Disinfect workstation and arrange in proper order

30 mins
Suggested Salon Speed

My Speed
_____
_____
_____

INSTRUCTIONS:

Record your time in comparison with the suggested salon speed. Then, list here how you could improve your performance.

_____
_____
_____
_____
_____

DARK SKIN EVENING MAKEUP

Why do manufacturers need to develop such a wide range of makeup colors?

INSPIRE

The ability to choose makeup colors for dark skin will allow you to adapt your techniques on all skin tones.

ACHIEVE

Following this *Dark Skin Evening Makeup Workshop*, you'll be able to:

>> Demonstrate proper procedures to perform a dark skin makeup design

PERFORMANCE GUIDE

DARK SKIN EVENING MAKEUP

View the video, then perform this workshop. Complete the self-check as you progress through the workshop.

30 mins
Suggested
Salon Speed

PREPARATION	✔
>> Assemble tools, supplies and products >> Set up workstation >> Wash your hands	☐

CLIENT/SKIN PREPARATION

1. **Cleanse, tone, moisturize and protect skin.** ☐

2. **Analyze skin and facial features.** ☐

3. **Drape client and position head band.** ☐

4. **Groom brows if needed.** ☐

5. **Select concealer and foundation color.** ☐

   Note: Refer to *Day Makeup Workshop* for steps 1-5.

FACE – CONCEALER AND FOUNDATION

6. **Apply concealer with brush to even out skin tones:** ☐

   >> Around inner eye, corner of nose, sides of mouth
   >> Use minimal pressure

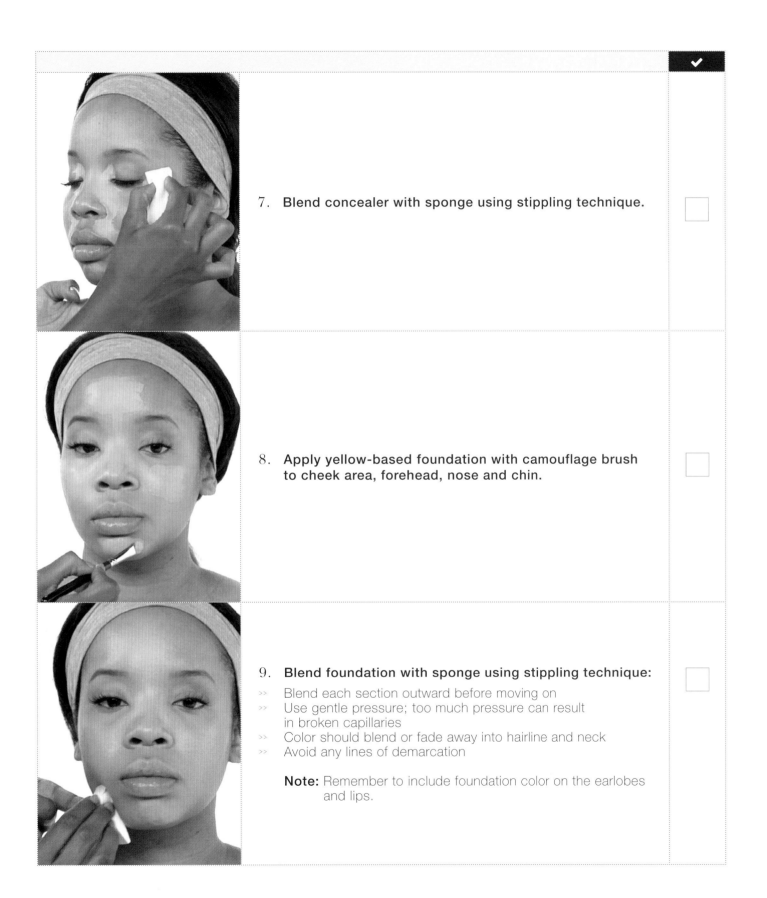

7. **Blend concealer with sponge using stippling technique.**

8. **Apply yellow-based foundation with camouflage brush to cheek area, forehead, nose and chin.**

9. **Blend foundation with sponge using stippling technique:**
   >> Blend each section outward before moving on
   >> Use gentle pressure; too much pressure can result in broken capillaries
   >> Color should blend or fade away into hairline and neck
   >> Avoid any lines of demarcation

   Note: Remember to include foundation color on the earlobes and lips.

EYES — BROW PENCIL AND EYE SHADOW ✔

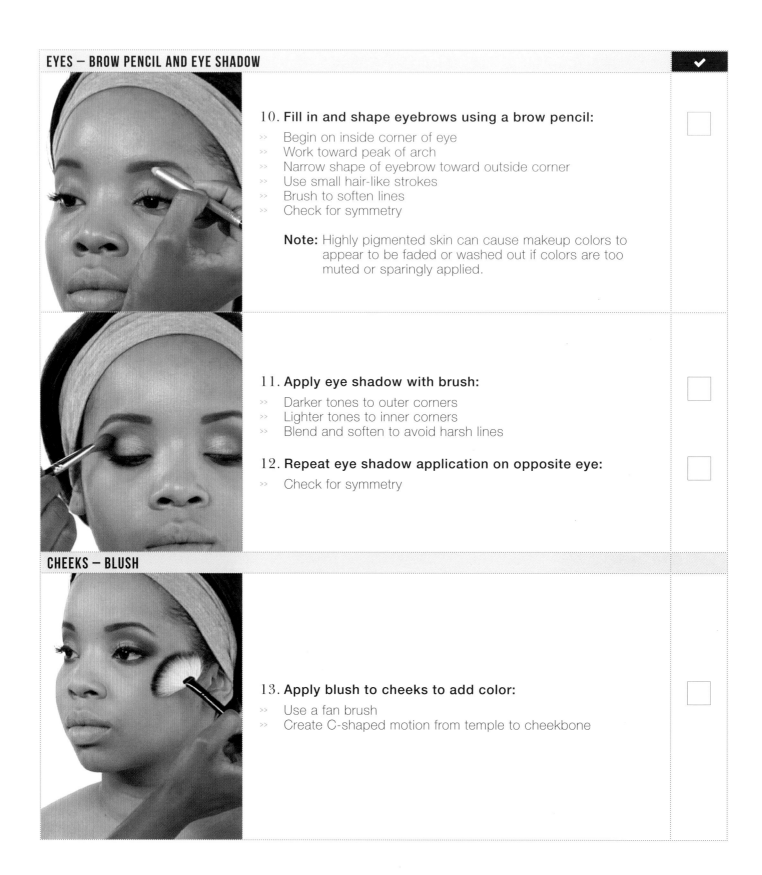

10. Fill in and shape eyebrows using a brow pencil:
>> Begin on inside corner of eye
>> Work toward peak of arch
>> Narrow shape of eyebrow toward outside corner
>> Use small hair-like strokes
>> Brush to soften lines
>> Check for symmetry

Note: Highly pigmented skin can cause makeup colors to appear to be faded or washed out if colors are too muted or sparingly applied.

11. Apply eye shadow with brush:
>> Darker tones to outer corners
>> Lighter tones to inner corners
>> Blend and soften to avoid harsh lines

12. Repeat eye shadow application on opposite eye:
>> Check for symmetry

CHEEKS — BLUSH

13. Apply blush to cheeks to add color:
>> Use a fan brush
>> Create C-shaped motion from temple to cheekbone

14. **Redraw shape of lips with lipliner:**
    >> Draw inside natural lip if minimizing size of mouth is desired
    >> Use small strokes working from outside corner toward center
    >> Outline upper lip
    >> Outline lower lip

    Note: You may choose to brace the hand under the chin to steady the application.

□

15. **Apply and blend lip color to create a harmonious balance through the entire face:**
    >> Darker lip color can be used for a stronger, more defined mouth

□

COMPLETION

>> Discard single-use supplies
>> Disinfect tools and multi-use supplies
>> Disinfect workstation and arrange in proper order

□

30 mins
Suggested Salon Speed

My Speed
_____
_____
_____

INSTRUCTIONS:
Record your time in comparison with the suggested salon speed. Then, list here how you could improve your performance.

_____
_____
_____
_____
_____

➡➡ 112 GLOSSARY/INDEX

Concealer *100*
Makeup product used to even out skin tone; helps to correct facial imperfections.

Congenital *22*
Occurring at or before birth.

Conjunctivitis *24*
Referred to as pink eye; an inflammation of the transparent membrane that lines the eyelid and eyeball; characterized by itching and redness; spreads easily.

Contagious Disease *18*
Communicable by contact; also known as an infectious or communicable disease.

Contraindication *31*
Conditions or factors that serve as reasons to withhold certain treatments.

Cool Colors *89*
Colors that contain more blue tones within them.

Crusts *21*
Dried masses that are the remains of an oozing sore; the scab on a sore is an example of a crust.

Dermal Layer *9*
Underlying, or inner layer of the skin; also called dermis, derma, corium, cutis or true skin; made up of connective tissues; sudoriferous glands, sebaceous glands, sensory nerve endings and receptors, blood vessels, arrector pili muscles and a major portion of each hair follicle.

Dermal Papillae *9*
Small, nipple-like extensions of the dermal layer into the epidermis; they appear as epidermal or papillary ridges (fingerprints) and are located at the base of hair follicles.

Dermatitis *24*
Inflammatory disorder of the skin.

Dermatitis Venenata *19*
Allergic reaction to certain cosmetics or chemicals; the skin becomes red, sore or inflamed after direct contact with a substance; sometimes referred to as contact dermatitis.

Dermatology *4*
Study of the skin, its structure, functions, diseases and treatment.

Diamond Face Shape *91*
The diamond face has predominant width through the cheekbones with a narrow forehead and chin/jaw areas.

Dry Skin *15*
Characterized by signs such as peeling and flaking; chaps easily and has a general, all-over taut feeling; has fewer blemishes and is not prone to acne.

Duct Glands *10*
Canal-like structures that deposit their contents on the surface of the skin; part of the endocrine system.

Eczema *24*
Characterized by dry or moist lesions with inflammation of the skin; requires medical attention.

Effleurage *32*
A light, gliding, gentle stroking or circular movement made with the palms of the hands or pads of the fingertips; used to begin and/or end a treatment; often used on the face, neck and arms.

Electrolysis *62*
Permanent method of hair reduction that uses electric current to damage the cells of the papilla and disrupt hair growth; usually performed by a licensed professional called an electrologist.

Epidermis *6*
Outermost layer of the skin; also referred to as cuticle or scarf skin.

Epilation *57*
The removal of hair from under the skin at the follicle. Examples include waxing, tweezing, threading and laser.

Epithelial Cells *6*
Cells that cover and protect the inside of the body.

Esthetics *4*
Known as the process of cleansing, toning, moisturizing, protecting and enhancing the skin.

Etiology *18*
The study of the cause of a disease, disorder or condition.

Excoriation *21*
Mechanical abrasions or injuries to the epidermis; e.g., scratches to the surface of the skin.

Excretion *5*
The skin's ability to eliminate sweat, salt and wastes from the body, therefore, helping to remove toxins from the internal systems.

Exfoliation *29*
The process used to remove the outer layer of epidermal cells, revealing newer skin beneath.

Eyebrow Color *103*
Makeup product used to shade or fill in the brows.

Eyeliner *103*
Makeup product used to define and emphasize the shape and size of the eyes.

Eye Shadow *103*
Makeup product used to contour or highlight the eyes.

Eye Tabbing *104*
Process of applying a cluster of individual lashes to the client's own lashes.

Facial *14*
A skin care service offered to provide soothing and/or healing effects.

Facial Masks   33
Products applied to the skin to cleanse, hydrate, tighten pores, exfoliate reduce excess oil or offer nourishment; include clay/mud, cream, gel, modeling and paraffin (warm wax) masks.

Facial Powder   102
Makeup product primarily designed to "set" other makeup products so that they last longer without fading, streaking or rubbing off.

Facial Steamer   41
Machine that sprays warm, humid mist on skin to open pores for cleansing.

Fan Brush   39
Used to apply product on face or neck.

Fissures   21
Cracks in the skin; e.g., chapped lips.

Follicle   6
Cluster of cells in the upper layer of the skin; the cell cluster pulls the upper layer down with it, creating a tube-like pocket called the root sheath out of which the hair will grow.

Folliculitis   24
Infection in the hair follicles caused by bacteria, shaving or clothing irritation. It usually looks like a red pimple with a hair in the center.

Foundation   99
Makeup product used to create an even skin tone and uniform surface.

Freckles   20
Discoloration on the skin's surface commonly found on the face, neck and chest; considered macules.

Friction   32
Circular or wringing movement with no gliding used on the scalp or with a facial when less pressure is desired; applied with the fingertips or palms; a way in which the hair cuticle can be damaged by combing and brushing.

Furuncles   23
Boils; appear in the dermal layer and epidermis and are caused by an acute bacterial infection.

Galvanic Method   62
Method of permanent hair reduction that destroys the hair by decomposing the papilla; also known as multiple-needle process.

Gel Masks   33
Designed for dry skin types and sensitive skin; may contain botanicals and ingredients designed to calm and soothe.

Heart Facial Shape   91
The heart (triangle) face has a wider forehead with a narrow jaw or chin line.

Heat Regulation   5
Skin's ability to help maintain the body's temperature.

Herpes Simplex   20
Contagious, chronic condition characterized by a single vesicle or a group of vesicles on a red, swollen base.

High-Frequency Skin Care Machine   42
A machine that creates current that is thermal, or heat producing, and germicidal for treatment of the skin.

Hydration   30
The process of adding moisture to the skin.

Hyperhidrosis   24
Overproduction of perspiration caused by excessive heat or general body weakness; requires medical attention.

Hyperpigmentation   7
Pigmentation that occurs as a result of variables such as overexposure to UV rays, acne, injuries to the skin, hormones or other external factors.

Hypertrophies   25
New growths; overgrowths; excesses of skin.

Impetigo   24
Highly contagious bacterial infection that produces a honey-yellow, crusted lesion, usually on the face.

Inflammation   18
An objective symptom characterized by redness, pain, swelling and/or increased temperature.

Infrared Lamp   41
A lamp that provides a soothing heat that penetrates into the tissues of the body; softens the skin to allow penetration of product and increased blood flow.

Integumentary System   4
Consists of the skin and its layers.

Keratinization   8
The chemical conversion of living cells into dead protein cells.

Laser Hair Reduction   64
Hair reduction treatment that uses wavelengths of light to penetrate and diminish or destroy hair bulbs.

Law of Color   89
Out of all the colors in the universe, only three—yellow, red and blue, called primary colors—are pure.

Leukoderma   23
Describes hypopigmentation (lack of pigmentation) of the skin caused by a decrease in activity of melanocytes.

Lip Glosses   106
Makeup product used to add color to lips; imparts a shiny appearance to the lips; generally has less concentration of color than lipstick; has moisturizing properties.

Lipliner   106
Makeup product used to define natural shape of the lips or correct the shape.

Lipstick   106
Makeup product used to add color to the lips.

Macules   20
Discoloration appearing on the skin's surface; a freckle is an example of a macule.

Magnifying Lamp   41
Provides thorough examination of skin's surface using magnification and glare-free light.

Makeup   88
Application of products that add color, highlights, contours and other enhancements to the face.

Mascara *104*
Makeup product used to define, lengthen and thicken the eyelashes.

Massage *30*
A scientific method of manipulating the body by rubbing, pinching, tapping, kneading or stroking with the hands, fingers or an instrument.

Massage Cream/Oil *44*
Skin care product used to reduce friction and provide "slip" to the skin during massage.

Mechanical Exfoliation *29*
The superficial loosening and reduction of cells in the outer-most layer of the epidermis, including methods such as facial cloths, scrubs or a brush; also called manual exfoliation.

Melanin *12*
Pigment that gives skin and hair their color.

Melanocytes *7*
Cells that produce the melanosomes or pigment granules containing melanin that give color to the skin.

Melanoderma *22*
Any hyperpigmentation caused by overactivity of the melanocytes in the epidermis.

Melanosomes *7*
Packets of melanin.

Milia *23*
Pearly white enclosed keratin-filled cysts filled with sebum, dead skin cells and bacteria which form a hard ball beneath the outer layer of the skin.

Miliaria Rubra *24*
Prickly heat; an acute eruption of small red vesicles with burning and itching of the skin caused by excessive heat.

Modeling Masks *33*
Masks that are mixed with water and applied in a thick consistency to the face; these masks dry and harden to a rubber-like consistency, then can be pulled from the face in one piece; these masks seal the skin, locking in moisture and creating a firm, taut feeling.

Moisturize *28*
The act of applying hydrating products to make up for the unavoidable losses the skin sustains from aging and exposure to the environment.

Moisturizer *44*
Hydrates and protects the skin.

Moles *22*
Small brown pigmented spots that may be raised; hair often grows through moles but should not be removed unless advised by a physician.

Monochromatic Color *89*
Color scheme using the same color (with variations in value and intensity) throughout the makeup design.

Nevus *22*
Birthmark or a congenital mole; reddish purple flat mark; caused by dilation of the small blood vessels in the skin.

Normal Skin *15*
Characterized by a fresh and healthy color; a firm, moist and smooth texture; freedom from blackheads and blemishes; and does not appear oily.

Objective Symptoms *18*
Signs of a disorder or disease that are visible; e.g., pimples or inflammation.

Oblong Face Shape *91*
The oblong (rectangle) face is long, narrow and angular. The jawline is wide and almost horizontal.

Oily Skin *15*
Condition that has an all-over shiny look and/or rough texture with blackheads and enlarged pores.

Oval Face Shape *90*
The oval face is rounded, long and narrow; represents the ideal shape.

Papillary Layer *9*
Lies directly beneath the epidermis; rich in blood vessels and capillaries, which provide nutrients to the epidermis.

Papules *20*
Hardened red elevations of the skin in which no fluid is present; a pimple is an example of a papule.

Pathology *18*
The study of a disease.

Pear Face Shape *91*
The pear (trapezoid) face has a narrow forehead and a wide jawline.

Petrissage *32*
Light or heavy kneading and rolling of the muscles; performed by kneading muscles between the thumb and fingers or by pressing the palm of the hand firmly over the muscles, then grasping and squeezing with the heel of the hand and fingers; generally performed from the front of the head to the back; used on the face, arms, shoulders and upper back.

Protect *28*
The act of applying sunscreens to help shield the face from the damaging effects of exposure to the sun.

Protection *5*
The skin's ability to shield the body from the direct impact of heat, cold, bacteria and other aspects of the environment that could be detrimental to one's health.

Pseudofolliculitis Barbae *24*
Medical term for razor bumps or irritation following shaving.

Psoriasis *21*
Round, dry patches of skin, covered with rough, silvery scales; condition is chronic and not contagious.

Pustules *20*
Small elevations of skin similar to vesicles in size and shape but containing pus; a pimple with pus is an example of a pustule.

Reticular Layer *9*
The lowest layer of the dermal layer; in direct contact with the subcutaneous layer; contains fewer blood vessels; contains the collagen and elastin fibers that provide the skin with its strength and flexibility.

Rosacea 23
Chronic inflammatory congestion of the cheeks and nose observed as redness, with papules and sometimes pustules present; also called acne rosacea.

Round Face Shape 90
The round face has a low, round hairline and a short chin with a very rounded jawline.

Safety Data Sheets (SDS) 44
An information sheet designed to provide the key data on a specific product regarding ingredients, associated hazards, combustion levels and storage requirements; formerly known as Material Safety Data Sheet (MSDS).

Scales 21
Shedding dead cells of the uppermost layer of the epidermis.

Scars 21
Formations resulting from a lesion, which extend into the dermal layer or deeper, as part of the normal healing process; keloids are thick scars.

Seasonal Disease 18
Disease influenced by the weather.

Sebaceous Glands 10
Oil glands; partially controlled by the nervous system; sac-like glands that are attached to hair follicles; result in oily skin when an overabundance of sebum is produced by the glands.

Seborrheic Dermatitis 23
A common skin rash with redness and scaly, pinkish-yellow patches that have an oily appearance; usually affects the scalp.

Sebum 5
A complex secretion containing a high percentage of fatty, oily substances; mixes with the secretion of the sweat glands and spreads over the surface of the skin.

Secretion 5
A process by which substances are produced and discharged from a cell, gland or organ to perform a particular function.

Sensation 5
Feeling or perception generated by the nerve ending just under the outer layer of the skin that makes you aware of heat, cold, touch, pain and pressure; the reaction to a sensation is called a reflex.

Shaving 57
Hair removal method most often used when unwanted hair covers large areas, such as women's legs, using an electric shaver, clippers or razor.

Skin 4
The largest organ of the body that covers nearly 20 square feet of the body's surface and protects it from invasion from outside particles.

Skin Tags 22
Small elevated growths of skin.

Spatula 39
Implement used to remove product from container.

Squamous Cells 8
Cells with a flat, scale-like appearance; found in the palms of the hands and the soles of the feet (stratum lucidum).

Square Face Shape 91
The square face has a broad, straight forehead and hairline with a broad jawline; short and wide; it looks very angular, almost masculine.

Steatoma 23
Sebaceous cyst or wen; a subcutaneous tumor of the sebaceous gland filled with sebum.

Stratum Basale 7
Lowest or deepest level of the epidermis where mitosis or cell division takes place.

Stratum Corneum 8
Uppermost layer of the epidermis; the toughest layer, composed of keratin protein cells that are continually shed and continually replaced by new cells from below.

Stratum Granulosum 8
Layer of the epidermis below the stratum lucidum and above the stratum spinosum; in this layer the cells become more regularly shaped and look like many tiny granules.

Stratum Lucidum 8
Layer of the epidermis just below the stratum corneum; it is located on the palms of the hands and the soles of the feet where there are no hair follicles.

Stratum Spinosum 7
Layer of the epidermis just above the stratum germinativum; sometimes considered part of the stratum germinativum; includes cells that have absorbed melanin to distribute pigmentation to other cells.

Subcutaneous Layer (Tissue) 11
Adipose (fatty) tissue below the dermal layer of the skin; protective cushion for the skin; acts as a shock absorber to protect the bones and helps support the delicate structures, such as blood vessels and nerve endings.

Subjective Symptoms 18
Sign of a disorder or disease that is felt but not necessarily visible; for example, itching and burning.

Sudoriferous Glands 10
Controlled by the nervous system of the body; each gland consists of a coiled base and tube-like duct opening on the surface of the skin to form sweat pore; control and regulate body temperatures; excrete waste products; help to maintain the acidic pH factor of the skin.

Sugaring 61
Hair removal technique that uses a paste made primarily of sugar applied to the skin in a rolling motion.

Sun Protection Factor (SPF) 12
Rating system for sunscreen to determine how long one can stay out in the sun without burning.

Sunscreen 44
Skin care product that protects the skin from UV rays or sun exposure.

T-Zone 15
Oily residue of the skin on the forehead, nose and chin.

Tactile Corpuscles 9
Types of nerve endings responsible for sensitivity to light touch; found within the dermal papillae.

Tapotement *32*
Also called percussion or hacking; light tapping or slapping movement applied with the fingers or partly flexed fingers; used on the arms, back and shoulders.

Thermolysis Method *63*
High frequency/short-wave method of permanent hair reduction that involves inserting a single needle (probe) into the follicle.

Threading *61*
An ancient method of hair removal that utilizes 100% cotton thread that is twisted and rolled along the surface of the skin.

Tinea *24*
The medical term for ringworm; contagious fungal disease characterized by a red circular patch of blisters caused by a fungal vegetable parasite.

Tone *28*
The process of applying a water-based product to further cleanse the skin while bringing it to its normal pH; identifies the warmth or coolness of a color.

Toner *44*
Water-based product containing beneficial ingredients, such as skin-repairing substances and antioxidants to help to cleanse, soothe and smooth the skin while bringing it to a normal pH.

Triadic Color *89*
Color scheme using three colors located in a triangular position on the color wheel; often used for more vibrant makeup designs.

Tubercle *20*
Large papule; hardened red elevation of the skin with no fluid present.

Tumors *20*
Solid masses in the skin; may be soft or hard; may be fixed or freely movable; generally have a rounded shape; a nodule is a small tumor.

Tweezing *58*
Hair removal method that uses tweezers; process commonly used to remove unwanted hair from smaller areas, such as eyebrows, chin or around the mouth.

Ulcers *21*
Open lesions visible on the skin surface that may result in the loss of portions of the dermal layer and be accompanied by pus.

Vacuum *41*
Skin care equipment used to create mild suction; increases circulation to the surface.

Verruca *22*
Name given to a variety of warts.

Vesicles *20*
Fluid-filled elevations in the skin caused by localized accumulation of fluids or blood just below the epidermis.

Vibration *32*
Shaking movement; your arms shake as you touch the client with your fingertips or palms.

Vitiligo *23*
Characterized by oval or irregular patches of white skin that do not have normal pigment.

Warm Colors *89*
Colors that contain more red or yellow tones within them.

Waxing *59*
Temporary hair removal method in which the hair is physically removed from the follicle by applying soft or hard wax to skin, allowing the hair to adhere to the wax and finally pulling off the wax/hair.

Wheals *20*
A solid formation above the skin, often caused by an insect bite or allergic reaction; hives, also called urticaria, are an example of wheal lesions.

Wood's Lamp *41*
Lamp with ultraviolet light used for analysis of the skin surface and deeper layers to aid in determining skin treatment.

PIVOT POINT

>> **ACKNOWLEDGMENTS**

Pivot Point Fundamentals™ is designed to provide education to undergraduate students to help prepare them for licensure and an entry-level position in the cosmetology field. An undertaking of this magnitude requires the expertise and cooperation of many people who are experts in their field. Pivot Point takes pride in our internal team of educators who develop cosmetology, esthetics and nails education, along with our print and digital experts, designers, editors, illustrators and video producers. Pivot Point would like to express our many thanks to these talented individuals who have devoted themselves to the business of beauty, lifelong learning and especially for help raising the bar for future professionals in our industry.

EDUCATION DEVELOPMENT | **Janet Fisher** // **Sabine Held-Perez** // **Vasiliki A. Stavrakis**
Markel Artwell
Eileen Dubelbeis
Brian Fallon
Melissa Holmes
Lisa Luppino
Paul Suttles
Amy Gallagher
Lisa Kersting
Jamie Nabielec
Vic Piccolotto
Ericka Thelin
Jane Wegner

EDITORIAL | **Maureen Spurr** // **Wm. Bullion** // **Deidre Glover**
Liz Bagby
Jack Bernin
Lori Chapman

DESIGN & PRODUCTION | **Jennifer Eckstein** // **Rick Russell** // **Danya Shaikh**
Joanna Jakubowicz
Denise Podlin
Annette Baase
Agnieszka Hansen
Kristine Palmer
Tiffany Wu

PROJECT MANAGEMENT | **Jenny Allen** // **Ken Wegrzyn**

DIGITAL DEVELOPMENT | John Bernin
Javed Fouch
Anna Fehr
Matt McCarthy
Marcia Noriega
Corey Passage
Herb Potzus

Pivot Point also wishes to take this opportunity to acknowledge the many contributors and product concept testers who helped make this program possible.

INDUSTRY CONTRIBUTORS

Jeanne Braa Foster
Dr. Dean Foster
Eyes on Cancer

Linda Burmeister
Esthetics

Mandy Gross
Nails

Andrea D. Kelly, MA, MSW
University of Delaware

Rosanne Kinley
Infection Control
National Interstate Council

Lynn Maestro
Cirépil by Perron Rigot, Paris

Andrzej Matracki
World and European
Men's Champion

MODERN SALON

Rachel Molepske
Look Good Feel Better, PBA
CUT IT OUT, PBA

Peggy Moon
Liaison to Regulatory and Testing

Robert Richards
Fashion Illustrations

Clif St. Germain, Ph.D
Educational Consultant

Andis Company

International Dermal Institute

HairUWear Inc.

Lock & Loaded Men's Grooming

PRODUCT CONCEPT TESTING

Central Carolina
Community College
Millington, North Carolina

Gateway Community Colleges
Phoenix, Arizona

MC College
Edmonton, Alberta

Metro Beauty Academy
Allentown, Pennsylvania

Rowan Cabarrus Community
College
Kannapolis, North Carolina

Sunstate Academy of
Cosmetology and Massage
Ft. Myers, Florida

Summit Salon Academy
Kokomo, Indiana

TONI&GUY Hairdressing Academy
Costa Mesa, California
Plano, Texas

Xenon Academy
Omaha, NE
Grand Island, NE

LEADERSHIP TEAM

Robert Passage
Chairman and CEO

Robert J. Sieh
Senior Vice President,
Finance and Operations

Judy Rambert
Vice President, Education

Kevin Cameron
Senior Vice President,
Education and Marketing

R.W. Miller
Vice President, Domestic Sales
and Field Education

Jan Laan
Vice President, International
Business Development

Katy O'Mahony
Director, Human Resources

In addition, we give special thanks to the North American Regulating agencies whose careful work protects us as well as our clients, enhancing the high quality of our work. These agencies include Occupational Health and Safety Agency (OSHA) and the U.S. Environmental Protection Agency (EPA). *Pivot Point Fundamentals*™ promotes use of their policies and procedures.

Pivot Point International would like to express our SPECIAL THANKS to the inspired visual artisans of Creative Commons, without whose talents this book of beauty would not be possible.